Agency in Teacher Supervision and Mentoring

Offering an in-depth examination of field supervision and the role of the university supervisors in preparing teachers, this book addresses the challenges of providing novice teachers with quality supervision through the support and guidance of teacher education programs. Through a research-based lens, Bates and Burbank discuss the role, responsibilities, and opportunities of the university supervisor. Critically examining the supervisor as an agent of change who is positioned to empower early career teachers, the authors dissect the necessary preparation and support new teachers need in contemporary P–12 classrooms.

Alisa J. Bates is Interim Dean of the College of Education at Concordia University–Portland, USA.

Mary D. Burbank is Assistant Dean for Teacher Education at the University of Utah, USA.

Routledge Research in Teacher Education

The Routledge Research in Teacher Education series presents the latest research on Teacher Education and also provides a forum to discuss the latest practices and challenges in the field.

Intercultural Communicative Competence in Educational Exchange
A Multinational Perspective
Alvino E. Fantini

Teachable Moments and the Science of Education
Greg Seals

Dimensions and Emerging Themes in Teaching Practicum
A Global Perspective
Edited by Melek Çakmak and Müge Gündüz

Teaching, Learning, and Leading with Schools and Communities
Field-based Teacher Education
Edited by Amy Heineke and Ann Marie Ryan

Teacher Education in the Trump Era and Beyond
Preparing New Teachers in a Contentious Political Climate
Edited by Laura Baecher, Megan Blumenreich, Shira Eve Epstein, and Julie R. Horwitz

Values and Professional Knowledge in Teacher Education
Nick Mead

Agency in Teacher Supervision and Mentoring
Reinvigorating the Practice
Alisa J. Bates and Mary D. Burbank

For more information about this series, please visit: www.routledge.com/Routledge-Research-in-Teacher-Education/book-series/RRTE

Agency in Teacher Supervision and Mentoring
Reinvigorating the Practice

Alisa J. Bates and Mary D. Burbank

NEW YORK AND LONDON

First published 2019
by Routledge
711 Third Avenue, New York, NY 10017

and by Routledge
2 Park Square, Milton Park, Abingdon, Oxon, OX14 4RN

*Routledge is an imprint of the Taylor & Francis Group,
an informa business*

© 2019 Taylor & Francis

The right of Alisa J. Bates & Mary D. Burbank to be identified
as editor of this work has been asserted by them in accordance
with sections 77 and 78 of the Copyright, Designs and Patents
Act 1988.

All rights reserved. No part of this book may be reprinted
or reproduced or utilised in any form or by any electronic,
mechanical, or other means, now known or hereafter invented,
including photocopying and recording, or in any information
storage or retrieval system, without permission in writing from
the publishers.

Trademark notice: Product or corporate names may be
trademarks or registered trademarks, and are used only for
identification and explanation without intent to infringe.

Library of Congress Cataloguing-in-Publication Data
A catalog record for this book has been requested

ISBN: 978-0-415-78821-2 (hbk)
ISBN: 978-1-315-22549-4 (ebk)

Typeset in Sabon
by Apex CoVantage, LLC

For those who use their agency to support educators in all contexts.

Contents

Acknowledgments	viii
Contributor Biographies	ix
Introduction: Reinvigorating the Practice of Supervision	1
1 Teacher Preparation in the United States	11
2 The Role of the University Supervisor and Teacher Mentor	26
3 Supervision as an Informed Craft	47
4 Technology Integration in Supervision	64
5 Leadership and Professional Development	84
6 Agency as a Means for Building Resilience	100
7 Supervision and Mentoring: Applications for Teacher Educators and Administrators	113
8 Conclusion	130
Index	141

Acknowledgments

From Alisa: Many thanks to the faculty and staff of Concordia University who supported this project with their enthusiastic encouragement. With gratitude to my parents for pitching in at home while I pursued this project. And to Jim, Laurel, and Tessa for the time spent away from the family while focused on the writing.

From Mary: To Matt and special thanks to Malynda for her technical support.

Contributor Biographies

Alisa J. Bates is the Associate Dean and Professor in the College of Education at Concordia University in Portland, Oregon. Dr. Bates began her career as an elementary teacher before moving into higher education and teacher preparation. Prior to coming to Concordia University in 2014, Dr. Bates was an Associate Professor and the Director of the Online MAT program at Willamette University, where she received the Lawrence D. Cress Award for Excellence in Faculty Scholarship, and an Assistant Professor at the University of Utah. Her scholarly agenda includes work in university supervision of field experiences, teacher research and inquiry, as well as effective online learning practices. In program development, Dr. Bates has designed numerous teacher education programs utilizing a clinical model approach for teacher learning and professional growth. Dr. Bates uses her agency to support high-quality, intellectual professional experiences for preservice and in-service teachers, empowering them in their roles as educated professionals.

Mary D. Burbank is the Assistant Dean for Teacher Education and Director of the Urban Institute for Teacher Education at the College of Education at the University of Utah. A faculty member since 1994, she holds the rank of Clinical Professor. She is a recipient of a 2014 University of Utah Diversity Award, a 2005 Distinguished Teaching Award, a 2002 College of Education Teaching Award, and service awards from the College of Education, University Alumni Association, and the community. Her teaching, research, and service interests examine pathways to higher education for underrepresented students and families with collaborations in math and science, including serving as a primary investigator on a 2010 Noyce grant. She is the author/coauthor of three books and has written multiple book chapters and peer-reviewed research articles. She has secured over $2.3 million dollars in federal and state grants and awards. She oversees accreditation for the university's teacher education programs.

Introduction
Reinvigorating the Practice of Supervision

At some point during a teacher's career, the teacher will have an experience with supervision or mentoring that will affect their ongoing evolution as an educator. These exchanges can be positive or negative moments that shape how the teacher makes sense of themselves, their practice, their engagement in professional learning, or their commitment to stay in the profession. For most teachers, mentoring begins during educator preparation, with support provided to teacher candidates during field experiences. "In one-on-one mentoring relationships, student teachers make meaning about their earliest teaching experiences and make decisions about their practice, which, [. . .], can profoundly shape their pedagogical development, view of the profession, and agency as educators" (Bieler, 2010, p. 422). Candidates who are successful and well supported in these early relationships are positioned to be empowered educators. A teacher's reflective perception of the value of that support directly relates to how those first experiences reinforce their sense of success in the role. Then, as a newly hired teacher, additional layers of supervision are included in the daily work through oversight by school and district administrators, and through formal or informal mentoring programs offered to new faculty.

While many question the value and purpose of teacher education as an entry to the career (Zeichner, 2018), supervision and mentoring are crucial scaffolds in teacher education and ongoing professional growth that influence teachers beyond that commonly considered in the context of teacher agency. Our view of teaching is one where "teachers must learn to be inquirers who can make connections between the theory and methods that are available to them and the practical situations they encounter in differing contexts" (Cohn & Gellman, 1988, p. 1). Teaching is more than technical practice and requires "adaptive expertise so that [teachers] are able to exercise their discretion and judgment in the classroom to adjust their teaching to meet the varied needs of their students" (Zeichner, 2018, p. 29). To instruct in this manner, the notion of teacher as professional (Zeichner, 2018) requires support from others in collaboration to improve practice, to identify linkages between theory and practice, and

2 Introduction

to encourage actions designed to foster continued growth and reflection. Together, these elements support practice rather than replicate instruction or policy without question. Teaching, learning, and mentoring in these ways facilitate the development of teacher agency and encourage ongoing growth in schools.

Supervisors as Change Agents for Quality Teacher Preparation and Mentoring

University supervision has traditionally been viewed as a fixed practice that includes several repetitions of the observation cycle: visiting the classroom, observing the student teacher, and providing feedback; then evaluating the student teacher at the end of the term. However, the reality of student teaching supervision is far more nuanced and complicated. Attention to the personal and emotional needs of each student teacher informs the context and flow of the observation cycle and may direct attention toward developing the whole teacher (as opposed to only instructional or management practices) as supervisors seek to help candidates transition from the student identity to the teacher identity. The developmental demands of each student teacher vary, and the intersection of their individual situation with the unique aspects of the context, the needs of the children, and the expectations of the cooperating teacher create a perfect storm of particular outcomes for a setting. Layered on this interplay of the teacher and context are the supervisory stance and personal and professional backgrounds of the supervisor, as well as the resulting intersections of the experiences of the supervisor with the teacher and novice. If we seek more from teaching than the simple replication of the curriculum, instruction, management, etc., then we must attend to the contextual elements that are informing each teacher's journey through change and the unique and varied identities of supervisors and mentors. The reality is that many early teacher mentoring programs also feature the typical cycles of observation and feedback first introduced in teacher preparation, so the complexities that apply during that time continue to apply in the early years of the teaching career.

Supervisors play a crucial role in fostering the development of teachers as change agents able to design and implement improvement in school settings. Incorporating the habits, skills, and knowledge to engage teaching as an act of change begins in teacher preparation and encourages teachers to see themselves as empowered and capable of growth—transforming themselves, their practice, the lives of their students, and the school and district as a result. Teacher preparation leans heavily on the university supervisor to help candidates make sense of what they have learned in university courses and how that information supports the work that happens in schools daily. Supervisors are able to witness the connections and misalignments between university theory and school practice as student teachers seek to work through the tensions with fidelity to the learning opportunities they want to provide to students. In this position of access, supervisors provide candidates with the opportunity to reflect on the apparent and less apparent, attend to areas for growth, justify the choices made with ongoing reflection, and encourage continued advocacy for each teacher's practical commitments and philosophical values. The same is true for mentors who seek to support teachers during the early career years as they provide the sounding board for safe reflection on both areas of strength and weakness.

To support this type of growth and development in teachers, supervisors also need to be agents of change—empowered through their own agency to bring supports to teachers in learning to reflect and grow their practice. "The process of facilitating change [. . .] is in itself a form of discovery learning whereby new understandings are shaped by the interchange of inside and outside, and by old and new experiences and habits of mind" (Rust & Freidus, 2001, p. 11). Supervisors change and grow as much as they influence change in others—the process of learning to teach encourages continued growth on the parts of all involved, including the student teacher, the cooperating teacher, and the university supervisor. Agency for supervisors requires that structures and systems are in place to encourage this complex practice. To better understand teacher and supervisor agency, a brief outline of our conceptualization of agency is needed.

Agency in Supervisors: How Is It Defined and What Does It Mean?

The concept of teacher agency arises from the school improvement models of the 1980s and early 1990s (Glatthorn, 1992; Rust & Freidus, 2001). Instead of passing ideas from the top down, the goal shifted to become focused more on helping teachers to become invested in school improvement from the bottom up, sometimes with the support of an external change agent provided to facilitate innovation (Rust & Freidus, 2001). "Teacher empowerment begins with teacher knowledge" (Glatthorn, 1992, p. 9), which can then facilitate the ongoing development of school changes that are driven by the inclusion, and often leadership, of teachers in the process. Teachers are invested with the power and responsibility to engage in their own professional development, collaborating with colleagues and other school staff to embed professional learning in the context of the school and classroom setting (Glatthorn, 1992). This focus on the contextual nature of school improvement recognizes the social construction of knowledge and the crucial, collaborative role teachers play in improving the practice of their own classrooms and schools (Hargreaves, 1996; Rust & Freidus, 2001). Further, "developing and sustaining a sense of agency in the classroom is a critical part of

4 *Introduction*

teacher fulfillment and retention" (Flessner, Miller, Patrizio, & Horwitz, 2012, p. 2). Critical behaviors such as these must be encouraged to foster ongoing investment in the profession.

One dimension of teacher agency has come to the forefront through the curriculum development process. Research in curriculum development has explored the role of agency in identifying how teacher empowerment is—or is not—enacted in the daily work of the classroom (Paris, 1993). Over time, the role of the teacher in curriculum development has shifted and changed with increasing attention to scientific efficiency in curriculum design, the desire for social efficiencies as school population and the teaching force explode in size, and the shift to a primarily female teaching force (Paris, 1993). Late in the 20th century active calls for the increased involvement of teachers in the curriculum process began to resonate; this period in history resulted in shifting teachers who were previously far less involved in the development or design of curriculum into active, visible players beyond their own classrooms.

However, over time teachers have moved from the role of "implementers" of curriculum to a more crucial responsibility as reform agents (Paris, 1993). While teachers are theoretically able to manipulate the curriculum they teach, movements towards greater standardization across classrooms, districts, states, and the nation have made it much more of a practical challenge. The current assumptions that drive curriculum development reinforce the role of the teacher as a passive participant in the work of curriculum and instruction—representing teachers on curriculum committees, serving as teacher representatives when selecting curriculum resources for adoption by a school district, and so on. These choices about teacher participation in the work of curriculum generation reinforce the notion that teachers are passive receivers and transmitters of curriculum to students and not active participants in the creation or implementation of curriculum in the classroom (Paris, 1993). This reinforces a lack of teacher agency despite the fact that the system perceives itself to be increasing and encouraging teacher agency through representation and inclusion in the processes.

At the same time as these curriculum models were dominating school practice, researchers reported on increasing agency of teachers in small pockets in the research across a variety of topics. For example, Cochran-Smith and Lytle's (1993) work on teacher research demonstrated teachers seeking to actively improve practice through the re-creation of curriculum as a result of their research. Paris (1993) further defines agency through teachers' relationship to curriculum that results in "personal initiative and intellectual engagement" (p. 16), incorporating the notion of moral responsibility and hesitancy to acquiesce for the sake of agreement. Agency arises from action (Paris, 1993; Greene, 1978) and incorporates action with others to promote growth of the community (Arendt, 1958;

Paris, 1993). Agency may or may not be officially sanctioned by administrators or the district, and the elements of "de facto agency" (Paris, 1993, p. 147) may result in greater ownership for practical outcomes and satisfaction on the part of the teacher. Paris (1993) cautions us that to support teacher agency, we must:

> recognize the personal, practical, and contextualized [. . .] knowledge that teachers already possess, to value the processes by which they create and critique it, and be sensitive to and build upon that knowledge and those processes that may already exist within teachers' repertoires.
>
> (p. 151)

Effective change agents influence and are influenced by the context of the focus situation (Rust & Freidus, 2001) and the relevant relationships. Contexts are evolving and diverse in the work of education, resulting in a need for supervisors to be closely in tune with the dynamics around them. Because of a layered influence, both insiders and outsiders within school contexts have the potential to be change agents impacting the outcome of the work but also impacting their own role as a participant. Rust and Freidus (2001) lay out three contributions of each participant: each "brings his or her unique expertise to the process, learns with and from others, and engages in identifying ways to meet the needs of the children and adults in the setting" (p. 4). These contributions facilitate agency in the participants by honoring their voices and perspectives.

Rust and Freidus (2001) identify four critical roles of change agents that arise from the research on different aspects of change. These roles include "negotiators, nurturers, teachers and learners, and curriculum developers" (p. 6). Each of these will be described to set the stage for consideration of the four influences as a part of mentoring and then addressed in terms of connection to supervision and mentoring throughout the text.

Negotiators

Collaboration requires negotiation; successful collaboration requires thoughtful and careful negotiation that leaves each party feeling heard, validated, and supported. As a change agent, the primary use of negotiation is to ensure that collaboration has the structure and plans for action necessary for success. Mandates offer little support for encouraging agency (Rust & Freidus, 2001) and negotiation must instead be completed to explore how the process will play out and the intended outcomes achieved. Supervisors, as negotiators, play a role in helping novice educators problem solve how to navigate change in school settings.

6 Introduction

Nurturers

Change agents must invest in relationships with others to ensure there is the trust and space for learning and growing (Rust & Freidus, 2001). Nurturing these relationships is fundamental for any exploration or reflection as this process of change is powerful, complex, and sometimes painful. Developing nurturing capacities for building relationships is crucial in one who will act as a change agent and requires attention to the personal and professional experiences that inform the approach one takes when working with other adult learners (Rust & Freidus, 2001). Supervisors and mentors are either successful or not in their role based on the relationships they develop with novice educators. Poor relationships are a nonstarter when looking to model and teach agency to others.

Teacher and Learner

Leading and learning with adults requires a different skill set than those used with children, and when teachers become change agents there is a learning curve to developing the knowledge and skills in this new role. Recognizing the needs of adult learners, and recognizing the diversity of adult learners, is something that must be addressed. Learning to lead, inspire, and facilitate the learning of adults requires development of a skill set that can support truly empowering change and innovation (Rust & Freidus, 2001).

Curriculum Change

Lastly, the change agents described by Rust and Freidus (2001) were focused on issues of encouraging teachers to enact curriculum and instructional changes. Throughout the stories shared, they identified that change agents who worked with teachers to impact growth were focused on both skill development and habits of mind that encouraged teachers to enact lasting change far beyond the moment of collaborating together. This required that the change agents possess deep knowledge of the innovations they supported, and contextual knowledge to support the teacher in the process of learning about improving practice. As such, supervisors must be up-to-date and facile in the other roles of change agents to facilitate teacher growth through curriculum change and innovation in practice.

Flessner and colleagues (2012) explored conceptualizations of agency in teacher education, looking closely at the ways that teacher educators define the concept. They identified three components that they felt were meaningful enactments of agency by teacher educators: agency as critical reflection, agency as contextualized activism, and agency as learning. In part, their intention was to "move the idea of agency and action beyond notions of empowerment to living spaces of thought, tension, and discovery" (p. xxi). Often, university supervisors realize this tension and discovery with preservice candidates as they interact around the challenges of teaching and learning in real-world contexts (Snyder & D'Emidio-Caston, 2001).

We have identified the following elements that are crucial to supervisor agency utilizing several different research sources (Bates & Burbank, 2008; Bates, Drits, & Ramirez, 2011; Bates, Ramirez, & Drits, 2009; Bates & Rosaen, 2010; Burbank, Bates, & Gupta, 2016; Burbank, Ramirez, & Bates, 2012; Rust & Freidus, 2001). Supervisors must possess and enact a professional sense of agency with novice educators. The characteristics of a supervisor who possesses agency include voice, a sense of empowerment, connectedness in educational spheres, an action-oriented approach, a reflective stance, and knowledge of best practices and educational contexts. A supervisor with agency:

1. Possesses a strong understanding of their individual supervisory stance and is able to enact this stance to inform work with novice educators;
2. Facilitates professional systems and models that encourage ongoing reflection about practice;
3. Utilizes advanced communication, collaboration, and relationship skills to encourage agency in teachers;
4. Supports innovation and best practices with novice educators; and
5. Pursues continual learning to improve supervisory practice.

To enact agency in practice with novice teachers, supervisors must be able to move beyond one-on-one relationships or small communities of teachers to speak for educators in professional circles both inside and outside of schools. To help supervisors achieve this complex, but crucial, model of supervision and mentoring requires systemic supports from teacher education programs, schools, districts, and states.

Effective Supervision: Looking Ahead to the Text

Effective supervision requires attention to the needs of the teacher and also to the needs of the supervisor. While there are many names in the field for the role of the university supervisor or early career mentor, for the sake of clarity we will use these two terms interchangeably throughout the text. In some cases, we may also refer to mentors as coaches when focusing on a particular responsibility or role enacted in the practice that reflects a purposeful coaching model. In "A Pivot Toward Clinical Practice, Its Lexicon, and the Renewal of Educator Preparation" (2018), the Clinical Practice Commission from the American Association of Colleges of Teacher Education advocates for clear and consistent language

8   *Introduction*

in practice across sites—a common lexicon that communicates a focused and purposeful understanding of what we mean when we reference a mentor, a student teacher, or a cooperating teacher. The intention here is to ensure that our terms reflect the capacity of the role and the complexity of the work that is undertaken by a supervisor beyond a sole emphasis on evaluation. As such, the text explores how these aspects of practice are present through diverse responsibilities of supervisors.

Chapter 1 provides the historical context for the work of supervisors and considers the current influences on practice. Supervision in the 21st century has been heavily impacted by the increased accountability measures mandated by schools, school districts, and states. Additionally, state and national accreditation efforts at the university level have changed the face of programs and practices related to supervision. This chapter looks at the history of teacher preparation and today's educational climate. It also considers current and potential outcomes for supervision while considering what supervisors might do to find a common ground between the need for individuality in teaching and the focus of the larger goals of accountability.

Chapter 2 provides an in-depth review of the literature on the relevance and practical programmatic structures of the university supervisor's critical role in a teacher preparation program. Specifics are provided regarding the research on the application of supervision approaches with adult learners, the role of reflection in teacher preparation (and the supervisor's involvement in this critical process), and current trends for support models that supervisors offer to preservice and early career teachers.

Chapter 3 focuses on the complexity of supervisory support as more than technical skills. Supervisors utilize background experiences, teaching beliefs, etc. to inform their theoretical and philosophical stances as they guide pedagogical decisions. These supportive, outsider influences are particularly critical in the context of today's schools in terms of diversity and intensity of curricular emphases. Calls for social justice in education and the need for equity in educational opportunity require a look at the support provided by supervisors and mentors in helping teachers to respond to these needs. Research from these areas develop the notion of supervision as a culturally responsive act in today's classrooms, looking specifically at language, curriculum, ability, and backgrounds as examples to build this understanding. Particular attention is directed at the context of supervision and the intersection of influences, such as teaching background on the practice of the supervisor/mentor. This chapter also examines the impact of content area disciplinary knowledge (e.g., math) and how content informs the type and form of supervision.

Chapter 4 considers technology integration in supervision. Technology plays an increasingly significant role in public education for both preservice and in-service teachers. This chapter explores how supervision harnesses this potential in an effort to build opportunities for mentoring and reflecting that are rich and facile for all parties. The chapter reviews the research on previous uses of technology and considers how new technologies might offer unique potential for maximizing the supervisory opportunities available for individuals and communities of practice.

Chapter 5 addresses leadership and professional growth through supervisory support and as a vehicle for advancement for supervisors and mentors. Student teachers and novice teachers practice in classrooms and schools with existing cultures, norms, and expectations for new members who join the community. This chapter considers the unique characteristics of leadership opportunities for mentors and supervisors, including the professional trajectory available to those engaged in this work. Features related to the contexts of schools and classrooms inform the type of relationships and practices mentors and supervisors establish in their work as classroom-based mentors.

Chapter 6 takes an in-depth look at the impact of student trauma and resilience on educator experiences. Given the increasing understanding about the impact of trauma on students' lives, both inside and outside of the classroom, and development (physical, emotional, social, and academic), teachers and mentors must both be equipped to address the impacts of secondary traumatic stress, compassion fatigue, and burnout. Supervisors play a powerful role in building relationships that buffer the impact of high-stress environments for novice educators, and this responsibility will be explored in Chapter 6.

Chapter 7 offers those preparing and guiding mentors and supervisors a number of recommendations for professional development to enhance a professional agency in their work as teacher educators. A discussion of research and historical trends will inform practical activities for reflection; self-studies within action research; examinations of school histories and contexts; explorations of teacher mentoring as part of accreditation and district requirements for preparation and professional development; and explicit recommendations for guiding work with novices.

Chapter 8 weaves together a number of issues from the text and explores how to make practical, real-world use of the ideas shared. It further proposes a variety of lingering questions and topics that might be used to continue the conversation in supervisory settings around the country.

References

American Association of Colleges of Teacher Education. (2018). *A pivot toward clinical practice, its lexicon, and the renewal of educator preparation.* Washington, DC: Author.

Arendt, H. (1958). *The human condition.* Chicago, IL: University of Chicago Press.

Bieler, D. (2010). Dialogic praxis in teacher preparation: A discourse analysis of mentoring talk. *English Education, 42*(4), 391–426.

10 Introduction

Bates, A. J., & Burbank, M. D. (2008). Effective student teacher supervision in the era of *No Child Left Behind*. *The Professional Educator, 32*(2), 1–11.

Bates, A. J., Drits, D., & Ramirez, L. (2011). Self-awareness and enactment of supervisory stance: Influences on responsiveness toward student teacher learning. *Teacher Education Quarterly, 38*(3), 69–87.

Bates, A. J., Ramirez, L., & Drits, D. (2009). Critical reflection in university supervision: Mentoring and modeling. *The Teacher Educator, 44*(2), 1–23.

Bates, A. J., & Rosaen, C. L. (2010). Making sense of classroom diversity: Supports for interns' learning about students through field instruction practices. *Studying Teacher Education, 6*(1), 45–61.

Burbank, M. D., Bates, A. J., & Gupta, U. (2016). The influence of teacher development on secondary content area supervision among preservice teachers. *The Teacher Educator, 51*(1), 55–69.

Burbank, M. D., Ramirez, L., & Bates, A. J. (2012). Critically reflective thinking in urban teacher education: A comparative case study of two participants' experiences as content specialists. *The Professional Educator, 36*(2).

Cochran-Smith, M., & Lytle, S. (1993). *Inside/outside: Teacher research and knowledge*. New York, NY: Teachers College Press.

Cohn, M. M., & Gellman, V. C. (1988). Supervision: A developmental approach for fostering inquiry in preservice teacher education. *Journal of Teacher Education, 39*(2), 2–8.

Flessner, R., Miller, G. R., Patrizio, K. M., & Horwitz, J. R. (2012). *Agency through teacher education: Reflection, community, and learning*. New York, NY: Rowman & Littlefield Education.

Glatthorn, A. A. (1992). *Teachers as agents of change: A new look at school improvement*. Washington, DC: National Education Association.

Greene, M. (1978). Teaching and the question of personal reality. *Teachers College Record, 80*, 23–35.

Hargreaves, A. (1996). Revisiting voice. *Educational Researcher, 25*(1), 12–19.

Paris, C. L. (1993). *Teacher agency and curriculum making in classrooms*. New York, NY: Teachers College Press.

Rust, F. O., & Freidus, H. (Eds.). (2001). *Guiding school change: The role of work of change agents*. New York, NY: Teachers College Press.

Snyder, J., & D'Emidio-Caston, M. (2001). Becoming a teacher of teachers: Two dilemmas in taking up preservice supervision. In F. O. Rust & R. Freidus (Eds.), *Guiding school change: The role of work of change agents* (pp. 102–120). New York, NY: Teachers College Press.

Zeichner, K. M. (2018). *The struggle for the soul of teacher education*. New York, NY: Routledge.

1 Teacher Preparation in the United States

Teacher supervision in the 21st century is influenced by daily work in classrooms and an ever-present focus on accountability compliance for schools, districts, and states. Within both teacher preparation and P–12 settings, program operations are impacted by a range of factors linked to accreditation and quality control for curricula, assessment, and supervisory practices. Tethered to these dimensions of school communities are understandings of the purpose of school and role of education. The implications for supervisors and mentors in their work with beginning teachers are far-reaching.

This chapter examines teacher preparation, including varied viewpoints on the purposes of schools. We consider the impact of contemporary views on mentoring and consider the role of supervision and actions designed to support the growth of teachers. We also explore the contexts of evolving and dynamic communities that acknowledge individual histories, the status of the profession, and the roles of increasingly diverse communities. School communities are complex and multifaceted. A recognition of the realities of educators' work and the roles of contexts illuminates the factors that impact decision-making and teacher empowerment. We situate a range of variables that impact reflective practice and their impact on the work of supervisors and those working in classrooms and schools.

Background

With few exceptions, varying viewpoints on the purpose(s) of schools remain central to professional discussions, opinion polls, and the increasingly frequent political rant! For most, personal perspectives on education are informed by the subtle and embedded factors within individual lives. Individual expertise regarding public education is influenced by myriad factors, including personal experiences and the range of national and local community perspectives and agendas on education. Coupled with beliefs regarding the purposes of schools are opinions on what constitutes teachers' work. For example, perspectives on the purposes of

12 Teacher Preparation in the United States

school may include generic descriptions of teaching and learning (Lortie, 2002). What we know from research and teachers' narratives is that life in classrooms is much more complex. To truly understand classrooms and schools requires an awareness of the inextricable linkages between education and the sociopolitical, economic, and bureaucratic features of communities. Mentors who acknowledge these dynamics are better informed in their efforts to create opportunities that foster agency when working with beginning teachers' holistic understandings of P–12 education.

Perceptions of education in the United States vary. For example, the purpose of school may reflect diverse beliefs regarding the roles of teachers, the influence of community insights on curriculum and assessment, and values regarding who is educated and in what formats (e.g., urban and rural communities, technology, children with diverse needs) (Langer Research Associates, 2016; Phi Delta Kappa, Gallup Poll, 2017). A 2011 survey of the public's attitudes on education found that 70% of Americans believed the ability to teach was more the result of innate talent rather than explicit training (Roth, 2014). Media portrayals fuel a profile of educators as either heroic martyrs (e.g., *Mr. Holland's Opus*) or bumbling villains (e.g., *The Simpsons*). Further, educators' work is sometimes viewed as so formulaic to the point where the teacher is practically irrelevant (Tucker, 1997). Components often overlooked in teachers' work include the nuances of pedagogy and assessment, recognizing learner differences, and understanding how these components impact teaching and learning.

Because teaching has been described as a melding of both the art and the science (e.g., Green, 2015), the technical components of teaching are one variable used to determine quality. Equally critical are dispositions among educators that inform relationship building and nuanced knowledge of learners (Danielson, 2007). Taken together, technical components of teaching and educator attitudes inform best practices and allow educators to facilitate student learning. Supervisors are in the unique position of supporting daily teaching and guiding professional development in ways that straddle the need for both data-based decision-making and reflection on practice. This goal is particularly challenging within a climate that narrowly defines profiles of quality teaching and its impact on evaluation of teachers' work, even when the national focus reflects an espoused commitment to educating every child (Brasel, Garner, Kane, & Horn, 2015; Every Student Succeeds Act, 2015; National Council on Teacher Quality, 2013, 2017).

For supervisors, the process of navigating contemporary educational terrain begins by building professional relationships that encourage reflection on practice. This task requires an understanding by mentors about the role of contexts, the climate of evaluation, and candid analyses of what is necessary for student learning in P–12 classrooms. Supervisor actions stemming from these broad-based understandings include oversight on professionalism, guiding and informing how educators approach curriculum and assessment, and facilitating how teachers respond to the ever-present changes in student demographics.

Complexities of Evaluating Teacher Quality in P–12 Classrooms

Similar to varied perspectives on the purposes of school, the assessment and evaluation of teachers' work is complex (Kraft & Gilmour, 2016; Weisberg, Sexton, Mulhern, & Keeling, 2009). Since the early 2000s, calls for preparing teachers have required greater specificity and rigor when determining quality. For organizations such as the National Council on Teacher Quality (2017), conversations on programs quality further narrow measures of accountability for those preparing future teachers. Dedicated attention to content area competencies and linkages between preparation and student performance are additional trends that delineate features of quality (Dillon & Silva, 2011; Kraft & Gilmour, 2016; Sawchuck, 2011).

Across time, various initiatives have been designed to offer seemingly fail-safe tactics for improving education quality by increasing standards, strengthening evaluation, and transforming curricula. The parameters of more recent legislation (e.g., Every Student Succeeds Act, 2015) illustrate attempts to ensure quality education for all learners with a specific focus on data-driven performance indicators (Heller, 2016). What is less clear are agreements on what constitutes quality and what these indicators might ensure.

Theoretically, efforts to measure teaching quality (e.g., knowledge of curriculum, assessment, and pedagogy) are designed to predict long-term impact of teachers' work on P–12 student performance. Further, measures such as content knowledge evaluations or classroom observations appear relatively appropriate for measuring quality (Eaton, 2011; National Council on Teacher Quality, 2013; Valli & Buese, 2007). However, beyond the nuances of content area preparation, effective programs must also include a defined program vision, attention to field experiences, and an established curriculum with attention to critically reflective practices (Ball & Forzani, 2010; Boyd, Grossman, Lankford, Loeb, & Wyckoff, 2009; Burbank, Ramirez, & Bates, 2016; Darling-Hammond, 2006, 2010; Harris & Sass, 2011). It is clear that determining teacher preparation programmatic impact is complicated, as assessment emphases and priorities are dependent upon a number of variables and stakeholders (Desimone & Long, 2010; Harris & Sass, 2011).

Research on teacher effectiveness highlights the complexities of assessment practices used to determine teacher quality (e.g., Donaldson & Papay, 2015; Rivkin, Hanushek, & Kain, 2005). For example,

14 Teacher Preparation in the United States

contemporary accreditation requirements recommend teacher preparation programs evaluate their graduates' impact on P–12 student performance using multiple measures such as performance data or perceptions of teacher effectiveness. These indicators are believed to demonstrate indicators of a preparation program's impact on teacher quality and effectiveness (e.g., Council for Accreditation in Education Preparation, 2017). While informative, these data points are also limited in that a range of factors impact P–12 student performance are outside the purview of teacher preparation. Features of instrumentation used to gather student performance data, assessment policies of districts and states, and characteristics of students and schools are among the variables. Data-based decision-making of teacher quality must also include examinations of how and why data are gathered for both teachers and students, with close reviews of the implications for daily practice (Kraft & Gilmour, 2016).

The challenge for teachers and their mentors is providing support that addresses both the philosophical and the practical demands of assessment and subsequent demonstrations of teaching "quality" (i.e., test scores). At times, these potentially conflicting demands may leave teachers and their mentors in the position of having to navigate disparate goals (Kraft & Gilmour, 2016; Voltz, Sims, & Nelson, 2010). These tensions are particularly challenging as supervisors search for greater clarity in their roles (e.g., university supervisor, mentor, coach, leader, or evaluator) and the related demands that blur lines between mentoring, supervising, and evaluating. Further complicating this work is keeping central the goals of fostering teacher agency and encouraging professional decision-making. A review of teacher preparation efforts provides an early look at the foundations from which educators begin their careers and offers supervisors a baseline in terms of how preparation impacts teachers' daily work.

Teacher Preparation Trends

Historically, gatekeeping responsibilities for teacher preparation have operated under the auspices of colleges and universities while coordinating with state departments of education. The traditional canon for teacher preparation has typically included a university-based curriculum and classroom-based experiences informed by standards and requirements for credentialing, as well as research on teaching and learning (Darling-Hammond, Holtzman, Gatlin, & Heilig, 2005; Lincove, Osborne, Mills, & Bellows, 2015). Contemporary accreditation mandates seek to further document teacher preparation through factors to include but not limited to: learner development and varied needs related to language, culture, and ability; assessment and data-based decision-making; managing classroom environments; and lesson planning and instruction (CAEP, 2017; NCTQ, 2017; NEA, 2011a, 2011b).

Teacher Preparation in the United States 15

In a climate where teacher shortages have changed the landscape in teacher preparation, challenges have been heightened in new and unexpected ways to ensure that preparation is comprehensive (Rich, 2015a, 2015b; Sutcher, Darling-Hammond, & Carver-Thomas, 2016).

These differences are noted when comparisons are made between traditional teacher preparation and contemporary alternative programs. Emphases on how teachers' work is viewed, the role of community engagement, and teacher leadership as professional decision makers are among the nuances within varied programs. For supervisors, varied goals and program efforts in teacher preparation bring a unique set of demands in their work. While these expectations for preparation are seemingly straightforward, educational communities must also consider whether the burgeoning number of alternative routes to teacher preparation abide by these beliefs and goals.

Custodial shifts in who prepares and ultimately monitors teacher preparation and teacher professional development have widened the preparation pool within the past 30 years. For example, alternative routes to teaching have emerged in response to market need, emphases on content area of specializations (e.g., math and science), and changes in the profiles of public education (e.g., charter and privatized P–12 education) (Lincove et al., 2015; Wayman, Foster, Mantle-Bromley, & Wilson, 2003). Alternate routes to licensure (ARL) have grown in popularity. To date, nearly all states have ARL programs; in 2016, reportedly up to 20% of teachers nationwide entered the field through an alternative route (DeMonte, 2015; Woods, 2016; Teacher Certification Degrees, 2017). While some practitioners, policymakers, and scholars have suggested that ARL programs are a valuable solution to address teacher shortage, others have decisively criticized them.

Empirical studies of ARL programs nationwide have reported wide variation in program requirements, implementation, and effectiveness (e.g., Scherer, 2012; Darling-Hammond, Chung, & Frelow, 2002; Goldhaber & Brewer, 1999; Grossman & McDonald, 2008; Kee, 2012; Qu & Becker, 2003), which may make program design and implementation comparisons difficult (Boyd et al., 2009). Limited pedagogical preparation within ARL programs is among the biggest criticism of many of these nontraditional routes (Wayman et al., 2003; Zeichner, 2016). Inadequate time in classrooms is also cited among many ARL programs and is a consistent concern, particularly because first-year teachers who arrive to the classroom underprepared are less effective and less likely to remain in the field (Clotfelter, Ladd, & Vigdor, 2006; Goldrick, Osta, Barlin, & Burn, 2012). Finally, for ARL program graduates, differences are manifest in retention rates, areas of expertise informed by their programs of study, and the ability to work with a range of students (Lincove et al., 2015).

Regardless of preparation experiences, the varied needs of beginning teachers create a unique set of challenges for supervisors, particularly

16　Teacher Preparation in the United States

because teacher preparation programs are not equal (Lincove et al., 2015). One issue is the need to provide teachers with the explicit support that effectively guides their skill development while encouraging the autonomy and agency necessary for quality teaching and professional advancement. In addition to support for teaching successfully, myriad factors impact how and why educators continue, and prosper, in their work. Without dedicated preparation, strong supervisory support, and ongoing attention to address the realities of today's classrooms, retention remains a challenge (Aragon, 2016; Papay, Bacher-Hicks, Page, & Marinell, 2017).

Classroom Diversity

Contemporary educators' work has moved beyond curriculum planning, lesson delivery, and assessment. Specifically, the daily work of educators requires an understanding of the culture of schools; the nature of teachers' work; the demands affiliated with assessment; standardization of the profession; and agendas for reform (e.g., Barth, 2002; Deal & Peterson, 1999; Cochran-Smith et al., 2012; Nichols & Berliner, 2007). Attention to an increasingly diverse community of learners is a particular area in which supervisory support is essential.

Like other complex systems, educators are situated in classrooms and schools that reflect a changing student population that is ethnically, culturally, and economically more diverse. For example, the integral role of contemporary communities and families as part of classroom life is now understood in ways not experienced by educators in the past (Dearing, Sibley, & Nguyen, 2015; Sibley & Brabeck, 2017). Work with increasingly diverse student populations for example, requires linkages to communities and family ambassadors as conduits for successful education experiences. As such, both veteran and new teachers may find themselves poorly prepared to consider how their curriculum, instruction, and assessment strategies meet the needs of the increasingly diverse and varied characteristics students bring to the classroom.

Research on student success reveals that teachers' deficit beliefs about students' language, ethnicity, gender, and socioeconomic status (SES) (Comber & Simpson, 2001; Weisman & Garza, 2002) often result in differential educational opportunities and limited success for marginalized students (Middleton, 2002). Therefore, it is incumbent upon supervisors to guide teachers' thoughts and practices to eliminate these limitations. The readiness of teachers to serve a range of students' educational needs is particularly critical as the population of P–12 linguistically diverse students expands.

Supervisors and Mentors: Teachers for Equity

But what about the skills and disposition of supervisors? In order for supervisors to support teachers in providing all students with the skills

Teacher Preparation in the United States 17

and opportunities for classroom success, mentors must possess the skills that allow them to reach these goals. As with the teachers with whom they work, these efforts are also dependent upon beliefs and skills that the supervisor has for serving all students in P–12 classrooms. Research into the impact of the supervisor's roles when working with diverse students reveal key areas mentors must address as part of their professional learning (Bates & Rosaen, 2010; Dantas-Whitney & Ulveland, 2016; Griffin, Watson, & Liggett, 2016). As such, supervisors and mentors are also expected to understand, guide, and inform teacher development in areas of diversity as they relate to expectations for teachers within various settings.

Teacher supervisors, similar to classroom teachers, reflect a demographic that is similar to the teaching profession (i.e., white and female) (Griffin et al., 2016) where within their preparation experiences, the majority of teachers now serving as mentors did not experience a focus on student diversity or social justice (Glimps & Ford, 2010; Hayes & Juarez, 2012; Liggett, 2014). Professional development for supervisors must take place for supervisors and mentors whose preparation as teachers took place well before current efforts to prepare teachers for dynamic and diverse communities. Both their experiences as teachers as well as their pedagogical training could be limited in areas related to diversity and social justice for today's classrooms and schools.

Research on preservice teacher supervisors' beliefs and perspectives stresses the critical importance of an approach that includes attention to teaching that supports all learners (Bates & Rosaen, 2010; Dantas-Whitney & Ulveland, 2016; Griffin et al., 2016). These authors cite the need for dedicated training and professional development for supervisors to ensure their guidance and mentoring reflect both the espoused mission of programs committed to social justice and the fundamental need to encourage equity in classrooms and schools for all learners. As these researchers note, those who mentor and supervise teachers must possess both the attitudes as well as knowledge of best practices for a wide range of learners.

The skills of an effective supervisor in a changing community must include both the knowledge of and ability to teach in ways that are culturally responsive and critically reflective (Gay, 2000; Grant & Sleeter, 2007; Villegas & Lucas, 2002). To assume that supervisors either possess or are limited in these dispositions and skills is remiss. Explicit attention to their training and evaluation in these areas is necessary to ensure that all supervisors are equipped to provide the support needed for the mentees to work with a range of learners in their classrooms (Bates & Rosaen, 2010; Griffin et al., 2016; Dantas-Whitney & Ulveland, 2016). It is necessary for dedicated programmatic attention and reflection on practices that provide opportunities to strengthen agency through supervisory support that is holistic and inclusive.

18   *Teacher Preparation in the United States*

Reflection Matters

A component of teaching and learning for *each player* in a supervisory relationship is the ability and willingness to reflect on current practices. For novices and veterans, and those responsible for their support, reflection is highly dependent upon belief systems regarding teachers' work (e.g., purposes of school, nature of learning, students, curriculum, assessment, etc.). Educators who understand the interplay between these dimensions of school possess the potential to think critically and reflectively (Clara, 2014; Schon, 1987; Shulman, 1987).

As a practice, reflection in education has rather deep roots, extending from early conversations on thinking that allow teachers to see their classrooms from multiple perspectives and in multiple ways (Dewey, 1933; Schon, 1987; Shulman, 1986, 1987). Reflective practices encourage attention to systems whereby teachers situate student achievement and motivation within contexts that impact classroom features, such as management. Through reflective practices teachers are able to effectively navigate curriculum and accountability demands in ways that promote teaching as more than a technocratic process (Clara, 2014; Kalchman, 2015). A central feature of this text is the role of reflection in enhancing agency and ownership in teachers' work.

While reflection on practice is typically viewed as valuable for teachers' work (Dewey, 1933; Schon, 1987), consideration must also be given to the impact of developmental differences among educators and their subsequent reflection on practice (Clara, 2014; Hayden & Chiu, 2015). That is, because novices and veteran teachers differ in the ways in which they approach teaching, supervisors and mentors must first understand their teachers as learners, and then respond to their mentees. Further, for mentors and supervisors, their knowledge of varied factors also impacts how lessons are perceived. It is essential that supervisors understand the range of teachers' needs, content areas, P–12 students, and contexts of classrooms that inform how they guide practice (Burbank et al., 2016). Situating problem-solving as a part of reflection on practice is a first step.

Contemporary research on reflection and its impact on teaching underscores an educator's abilities to thoughtfully examine both the big picture in education as well as the day-to-day practices that impact teaching and learning (Hayden & Chiu, 2015; Kalchman, 2015). Further, research on teacher development highlights a continuum of performance that often includes, but is not limited to, skill improvements, reflection on practice, and an awareness of broad-based factors that influence teaching and learning (Berliner, 1992; Dreyfus & Dreyfus, 1986). There is a tendency for novice teachers to focus teaching on the more rudimentary and skill-based components of lesson delivery. Teachers at this stage of their careers are often unaware or less skilled in their understanding of the relationships between the different variables

Teacher Preparation in the United States   19

in classrooms, including individuals and their histories (e.g., language, ability, and culture).

A dilemma for those working with teachers is recognizing and scaffolding both the practical and the conceptual skills required of teachers as they develop throughout their careers. For example, research on teaching and content area expertise delineates the types of knowledge used by educators that includes both teaching pedagogy as well as content (Burbank, Bates, & Gupta; 2016; Shulman, 1986, 1987). The nuances of knowledge types require complex feedback. Content knowledge, knowledge of pedagogy (i.e., instruction), and the unique pedagogical content knowledge are distinct curricular areas that require attention to explicit teaching competencies (Burbank et al., 2016; Shulman, 1986, 1987). It is therefore within the purview of supervisory and mentoring support to name the components of knowledge and instruction required for effective teaching as a way to increase teachers' competencies. In doing so, teachers' knowledge and reflection on dimensions of teaching and learning informs their agency in the classroom as teachers and leaders.

Supervisors' Work Within Complex and Layered Contexts

The implications for those working in supervisory and mentoring roles include deliberate conversations and analyses of teaching that challenge habits of practice among educators, while simultaneously providing alternatives designed to improve teaching. On a large scale, supervisors and mentors must be intentional in their guidance to provide beginning teachers with explicit support in ways that move their thinking beyond procedural knowledge (Allen & Casbergue, 1997; Wolf, Jarodzka, Van Den BoGert, & Boshuizen, 2015). In meeting these goals, supervisors are enhancing teacher agency in ways that move beyond skill acquisition. Further, supervisors must explicitly outline the contextual factors that influence actions within teaching episodes, pointing out cause-and-effect relationships across variables. Video-based evaluations of teaching are an increasingly useful method for these in-depth discussions of teaching moments (see Chapter 5).

Supervisors and mentors are in the position to offer concrete recommendations to teachers that are informed by research on student learning. These goals are met through guided practice with explicit references to research, coursework, or professional development (Hayden & Chiu, 2015). Supervisors who are knowledgeable of a range of factors are poised to direct feedback in ways that allow for teaching through problem exploration, adaptation of instruction, and the examination of methods for data collection using tools such as action research (Bullough & Gitlin, 2009; Clara, 2014; Cochran-Smith & Lytle, 1993; Zeichner & Liston, 1987). Mentors at the preservice level are in the position of

20   *Teacher Preparation in the United States*

teaching student teachers how to use individual lesson plans to build student engagement, understand the unique needs of learners, and customize assessment using multiple methods (e.g., questioning strategies, individual work, and work with others).

Conclusion

Supervisors in the 21st century require a complex and in-depth tapestry of dispositions and skills. Successful mentors are those whose knowledge of research-to-practice informs work in diverse and ever-changing classrooms and communities (Lucas & Villegas, 2011). Supervisors are situated as members of educational teams where classroom teachers, administrators, and the community work together in support of quality P–12 education. In their unique roles, supervisors are poised to finesse the necessary support and guidance that encourages teacher agency through reflection and informed decision-making. But these efforts must first begin with the mentors themselves. Like the teachers with whom they work, these educators must consider how ideologies, personal experiences in classrooms and schools, and expectations for quality will inform their work. This opportunity for mentors invites reflection and action toward the goal of serving P–12 students in the best possible ways.

References

Allen, R., & Casbergue, R. (1997). Evolution of novice through expert teachers' recall: Implications for effective reflection on practice. *Teaching and Teacher Education, 13*(7), 741–755.

Aragon, S. (2016). *Teacher shortages: What we know*. Education Commission of the States. Retrieved from www.ecs.org/ec-content/uploads/Teacher-Shortages-What-We-Know.pdf

Ball, D., & Forzani, M. (2010). What does it take to make a teacher? *Teacher Education, 92*(2), 8–12.

Barth, R. (2002). The culture. *Educational Leadership, 9*, 6–11.

Bates, A. J., & Rosaen, C. (2010). Making sense of classroom diversity: How can field instruction practices support interns' learning? *Studying Teacher Education, 6*(1), 45–61. doi:10.1080/17425961003669151

Berliner, D. C. (1992). The nature of expertise in teaching. In C. K. Osu, A. Dick, & J. L. Patry (Eds.), *Effective and responsible teaching: The new synthesis*. San Francisco, CA: Jossey-Bass.

Boyd, D. J., Grossman, P. L., Lankford, H., Loeb, S., & Wyckoff, J. (2009). Teacher preparation and student achievement. *Education Evaluation and Policy Analysis, 31*(4), 416–440.

Brasel, J., Garner, B., Kane, B. D., & Horn, I. S. (2015, November). Getting to the why and how. *Educational Leadership Online*. Retrieved from www.ascd. org/publications/educational-leadership/nov15/vol73/num03/Getting-to-the-Why-and-How.aspx

Bullough, R. V., & Gitlin, A. (2009). *Becoming a student of teaching*. New York, NY: Routledge Falmer.

Burbank, M. D., Ramirez, L., & Bates, A. J. (2016). The impact of critical reflective teaching: A rhetoric continuum. *Action in Teacher Education, 38*(2), 104–119.

Burbank, M. D., Bates, A. J., & Gupta, U. (2016). The influence of teacher development on preservice supervision: A case study across content areas. *The Teacher Educator, 51*, 55–69. doi:10.1080/08878730.2015.1107441

Clara, M. (2014). What is reflection? Looking for clarity in an ambiguous notion. *Journal of Teacher Education, 66*(3), 261–271. doi:10.1177/0022487114552028

Clotfelter, C., Ladd, H., & Vigdor, J. (2006). Teacher-student matching and the Assessment of Teacher Effectiveness. *Journal of Human Resources, 41*(4), 778–782.

Cochran-Smith, M., McQuillan, P., Mitchell, K., Terrell, D. G., Barnatt, J., D'Souza, L., & Gleeson, A. M. (2012). A longitudinal study of teaching practice and early career decisions: A cautionary tale. *American Educational Research Journal, 49*, 844–880.

Cochran-Smith, M., & Lytle, S. (1993). *Inside/outside: Teacher research and knowledge*. New York, NY: Teachers College Press.

Comber, B., & Simpson, A. (Eds.). (2001). *Negotiating critical literacies in classrooms*. Mahwah, NJ: Lawrence Erlbaum Associates.

Council for Accreditation in Education Preparation. (CAEP). (2017). Retrieved from http://caepnet.org/

Danielson, C. (2007). *Enhancing professional practice: A framework for teaching*. Alexandria, VA: Association for Supervision and Curriculum Development.

Darling-Hammond, L. (2010). Teacher education and the American future. *Journal of Teacher Education, 61*(1–2), 35–47.

Darling-Hammond, L. (2006). Constructing 21st-century teacher education. *Journal of Teacher Education, 57*(3), 300–314.

Darling-Hammond, L., Holtzman, D. J., Gatlin, S. J., & Heilig, J. V. (2005). Does teacher preparation matter? Evidence about teacher certification, Teach for America, and teacher effectiveness. *Education Policy Analysis Archives, 13*(42). Retrieved from http://epaa.asu.edu/epaa/v13n42/

Darling-Hammond, L., Chung, R., & Frelow, F. (2002). Variation in teacher preparation: How well do different pathways prepare teachers to teach? *Journal of Teacher Education, 53*(4), 286–302.

Dantas-Whitney, M., & Ulveland, R. (2016). Problematizing assumptions, examining dilemmas, and exploring promising possibilities in culturally relevant pedagogy: A response to "I didn't see it as a cultural thing": Supervisors of student teachers define and describe culturally responsive supervision. *Democracy & Education, 24*(1), 1–4.

Deal, C., & Peterson, K. (1999). *Shaping school culture*. San Francisco, CA: Jossey-Bass.

Dearing, E., Sibley, E., & Nguyen, H. (2015). Achievement mediators of family engagement in children's education: A family—school—community systems model. In S. Sheridan & E. M. Kim (Eds.), *Research on family—school partnerships, Vol. II: Processes and pathways of family—school partnerships* (pp. 17–39). New York, NY: Springer.

Desimone, L., & Long, D. (2010). Teacher effects and the achievement gap: Do teacher and teaching quality influence the achievement gap between Black and

22 *Teacher Preparation in the United States*

White and high-and low-SES students in the early grades? *Teachers College Record, 112*(12), 3024–3073.

Dillon, E., & Silva, E. (2011). Grading the teachers' teachers: Higher education comes under scrutiny. *Phi Delta Kappan, 93*(1), 54–58.

Donaldson, M. L., & Papay, J. P. (2015). Teacher evaluation for accountability and development. In H. F. Ladd & M. E. Goertz (Eds.), *Handbook of research in education finance and policy* (pp. 174–193). New York, NY: Routledge.

DeMonte, J. (2015). *A million new teachers are coming: Will they be ready to teach?* Washington, DC: Education Policy Center at American Institutes for Research. Retrieved from http://educationpolicy.air.org/sites/default/files/Brief-MillionNewTeachers.pdf

Dewey, J. (1933). *How we think: A restatement of the relation of reflective thinking and the education process.* Boston, MA: D.C. Heath.

Dreyfus, H. L., & Dreyfus, S. E. (1986). *Mind over machine: The power of human intuition and expertise in the era of the computer.* New York, NY: Free Press.

Eaton, C. (2011). Education Department's reform plan for teacher training gets mixed reviews. *The Chronicle of Higher Education, 57.*

Every Student Succeeds Act. (2015). *Department of education.* Retrieved from www.ed.gov/essa?src=rnay

Gay, G. (2000). *Culturally responsive teaching: Theory, research, and practice.* New York, NY: Teachers College Press.

Grant, C. A., & Sleeter, C. E. (2007). *Doing multicultural education for achievement and equity.* New York, NY: Routledge.

Glimps, B. J., & Ford, N. (2010). White power and privilege: Barriers to culturally responsive teaching. *International Journal of Educational Policies, 4*(1), 39–52.

Green, E. (2015). *Building a better teacher: How teaching works (and how to teach it to everyone).* New York, NY: W.W. Norton.

Griffin, L. B., Watson, D., & Liggett, T. (2016). "I didn't see it as a cultural thing": Supervisors of student teachers define and describe culturally responsive supervision. *Democracy & Education, 24*(1), 1–13. Retrieved from http://democracyeducationjournal.org/

Goldhaber, D., & Brewer, D. J. (1999). Teacher licensing and student achievement. In M. Kanstoroom & C. E. Finn, Jr. (Eds.), *Better teacher, better schools* (pp. 83–102). Washington, DC: The Thomas B. Fordham Foundation.

Goldrick, L., Osta, D., Barlin, D., & Burn, J. (2012). *Review of state policies on teacher induction.* Santa Cruz, CA: New Teacher Center. Retrieved from www.newteachercenter.org/sites/default/files/ntc/main/resources/brf-ntc-policy-state-teacher-induction.pdf

Grossman, P., & McDonald, M. (2008). Back to the future: Directions for research in teaching and teacher education. *American Educational Research Journal, 45*(1), 184–205.

Harris, D. N., & Sass, T. R. (2011). Teacher training, teacher quality and student achievement. *Journal of Public Economics, 95,* 798–812.

Hayden, E., & Chiu, M. (2015). Reflective teaching via a problem exploration, teaching adaptations, resolution cycle: A mixed methods study of preservice teachers' reflective notes. *Journal of Mixed Methods Research, 9*(2), 133–153.

Hayes, C., & Juarez, B. (2012). There is no culturally responsive teaching spoken here: A critical race perspective. *Democracy and Education, 20*(1), Article 1.

Teacher Preparation in the United States   23

Heller, R. (2016, October 11). ESSA and performance assessments: Where do states go from here. *Education Week*. Retrieved from http://blogs.edweek.org/edweek/learning_deeply/2016/10/moving_forward_on_performance_assessment_keep_an_eye_on_virginia.html

Kalchman, M. (2015). Focusing on reflective practice: Reconsidering field experiences for urban teacher preparation. *Perspectives on Urban Education, 12*(1), 3–17.

Kee, A. N. (2012). Feelings of preparedness among alternatively certified teachers: What is the role of program features? *Journal of Teacher Education, 63*(1), 23–38.

Kraft, M. A., & Gilmour, A. F. (2016). Can principals promote teacher development as evaluators? A case study of principals' views and experiences. *Educational Administration Quarterly, 52*(5), 711–753.

Langer Research Associates. (2016). *Critical issues in public education: The 2016 Phi Delta Kappa Survey*. Retrieved from http://hufsd.edu/assets/pdf/board/Phi%20Delta%20Kappa%20Annual%20Poll%20of%20the%20Public%27s%20Attitudes%20Toward%20the%20Public%20Schools.pdf

Liggett, T. (2014). Deliberative democracy in English-language education: Cultural and linguistic inclusion in the school community. *Democracy & Education, 22*(2), Article 4. Retrieved from http://democracyeducationjournal.org/home/vol22/iss2/4

Lincove, J., Osborne, C., Mills, N., & Bellows, L. (2015). Teacher preparation for profit or prestige: Analysis of a diverse market for teacher preparation. *Journal of Teacher Education, 66*(5), 415–434. doi:10.1177/0022487115602311

Lortie, D. C. (2002). *School teacher: A sociological study*. Chicago, IL: University of Chicago Press.

Lucas, T., & Villegas, A. M. (2011). A framework for preparing linguistically responsive teachers. In T. Lucas (Ed.), *Teacher preparation for linguistically diverse classrooms: A resource for teacher educators* (pp. 55–72). New York, NY: Taylor & Francis.

Middleton, V. A. (2002). Increasing preservice teachers' diversity beliefs and commitment. *The Urban Review, 34*(4), 343–361. Retrieved from http://link.springer.com/journal/11256

National Council on Teacher Quality (NCTQ). (2017). Retrieved from www.nctq.org/siteHome.do

National Education Association (NEA). (2011a). *English language learners face unique challenges*. Retrieved from www.nea.org/assets/docs/HE/ELL_Policy_Brief_Fall_08_(2).pdf

National Education Association (NEA). (2011b). *Professional development for general education, teachers of English language learners*. Retrieved from www.nea.org/home/42549.htm

National Council on Teacher Quality. (2013). *US news and world report*. Retrieved July 1, 2013, from www.usnews.com/education/nctq

Nichols, S., & Berliner, D. (2007). *Collateral damage: How high-stakes testing corrupts America's schools*. Cambridge, MA: Harvard Education Press.

Papay, J., Bacher-Hicks, A., Page, L., & Marinell, W. (2017). The challenge of teacher retention in urban schools: Evidence of variation from a cross-site analysis. *Educational Researcher, 46*(8), 434–448.

Phi Delta Kappa. (2017). *Gallup poll*. Retrieved from http://pdkpoll.org/

24 Teacher Preparation in the United States

Qu, Y., & Becker, B. J. (2003, April). *Does traditional teacher certification imply quality? A meta-analysis*. Paper presented at Annual Meeting, American Educational Research Association, Chicago, IL.

Rich, M. (2015a, August 10). Teacher shortages spur a nationwide hiring scramble (Credentials Optional). *New York Times*. Retrieved from www.nytimes.com/2015/08/10/us/teacher-shortages-spur-a-nationwide-hiring-scramble-credentials-optional.html

Rich, M. (2015b, April 12). Where are the teachers of color? *New York Times*. Retrieved from www.nytimes.com/2015/04/12/sunday-review/where-are-the-teachers-of-color.html?_r=0

Rivkin, S. G., Hanushek, E. A, & Kain, J. F. (2005). Teachers, schools, and academic achievement. *Econometrica*, *73*(2), 417–458.

Roth, M. (2014, September 5). Book review: 'Building a Better Teacher,' on secrets of good teaching by Elizabeth Green. *The Washington Post*.

Sawchuck, S. (2011, March 8). Administration pushes teacher-prep accountability. *Education Week*, *30*(23), 1, 14.

Scherer, M. (2012). The challenge of supporting new teachers. *Educational Leadership*, *69*(8), 18–23.

Schön, D. A. (1983). *The reflective practitioner*. New York, NY: Basic Books.

Schon, D. A. (1987). *Educating the reflective practitioner: Towards a new design for teaching and learning in the professions*. San Francisco, CA: Jossey-Bass.

Shulman, L. S. (1987). Knowledge and teaching: Foundations of the new reform. *Harvard Educational Review*, *57*(1), 1–22.

Shulman, L. S. (1986). Those who understand: Knowledge growth in teaching. *Educational Researcher*, *15*(2), 4–31.

Sibley, E., & Brabeck, K. (2017). Latino immigrant students' school experiences in the United States: The importance of family-school-community collaborations. *School Community Journal*, *27*(1), 137–157.

Sutcher, L., Darling-Hammond, L., & Carver-Thomas, D. (2016). *A coming crisis in teaching? Teacher supply, demand and shortages in the US*. Learning Policy Institute. Retrieved from https://learningpolicyinstitute.org/product/coming-crisis-teaching

Teacher Certification Degrees. (2017). Retrieved from www.teachercertificationdegrees.com/alternative/

Tucker, P. D. (1997). Lake Wobegon: Where all teachers are competent (or, have we come to terms with the problem of incompetent teachers?). *Journal of Personnel Evaluation in Education*, *11*(2), 103–126.

Valli, L., & Buese, D. (2007). The changing roles of teachers in an era of high-stakes accountability. *The American Educational Research Journal*, *44*(3), 519–558.

Villegas, A. M., & Lucas, T. (2002). *Educating culturally responsive teachers: A coherent approach*. Albany, NY: State University of New York Press.

Voltz, D., Sims, M., & Nelson, B. (2010). *Connecting teachers, students, and standards: Strategies for success in diverse and inclusive classrooms*. Alexandria, VA: Association for Supervision and Curriculum Development.

Wayman, J. C., Foster, A. M., Mantle-Bromley, C., & Wilson, C. A. (2003). A comparison of the professional concerns of traditionally prepared and alternatively licensed new teachers. *The High School Journal*, *3*(86), 35–40.

Weisberg, D., Sexton, S., Mulhern, J., & Keeling, D. (2009). *The widget effect: Our national failure to acknowledge and act on differences in teacher effectiveness.* Washington, DC: New Teacher Project.

Weisman, E. M., & Garza, S. A. (2002). Preservice teacher attitudes toward diversity: Can one class make a difference? *Equity & Excellence in Education,* 35(1), 28–34. doi:10.1080/713845246

Wolf, C., Jarodzka, N., Van Den BoGert, H., & Boshuizen, H. (2015). Keeping an eye on learning: Differences between expert and novice teachers' representations of classroom management events. *Journal of Teacher Education,* 66(1), 68–85.

Woods, J. R. (2016). Mitigating teacher shortages: Alternative teacher certification. *Education Commission of the States.* Retrieved from www.ecs.org/ec-content/uploads/Mitigating-Teacher-Shortages-Alternative-Certification.pdf

Zeichner, K. (2016). *Independent teacher education programs: Apocryphal claims, illusory evidence.* Boulder, CO: National Education Policy Center. Retrieved from https://files.eric.ed.gov/fulltext/ED574697.pdf

Zeichner, K., & Liston, D. (1987). Teaching student teachers to reflect. *Harvard Educational Review,* 57(1), 23–48.

2 The Role of the University Supervisor and Teacher Mentor

University supervisors function as key players in the implementation of teacher education programs in the schools by providing support for candidates' clinical experiences. They are often viewed as an agent of the university with an undertone of *evaluator, form completer*, and *enforcer* rather than as *mentor, facilitator, guide*, or other more constructive visions that really harness the potential of the university supervisor. As described in the introduction, the mentoring and support role is often undervalued in the broader scope of colleges of education, with relatively little emphasis placed on training, professional development, or ongoing support for the role and its functions. Supervisors typically get very little direction and guidance beyond the university's requirements, forms, and processes for documenting candidate learning. However, when considering the research on the triad (cooperating teacher, student teacher, and university supervisor) and the perspectives of student teachers, researchers have found that university supervisors play a valued part in the learning experiences of student teachers (Bates, Drits, & Ramirez, 2011; Gimbert & Nolan, 2003; Lee, 2011).

One of the critical elements of this work is attention to and understanding of both student teachers and mentors as adult learners. Facilitating growth and reflection in adult learners takes experience and understanding of how adults are both similar and different from children as learners. Because most supervisors come from educational backgrounds as former/retired teachers, former/retired administrators, or graduate students in education, the assumption is often made that because one knows how to teach children, one will be successful as a mentor of adults. However, this is not an appropriate automatic or logical assumption to be made given what is known about the unique needs of adult learners.

This chapter will explore the relevance of understanding adult learners, the traditional forms of supervision in teacher education, and the implications and outcomes of the common practices for supervisory practice. The chapter also discusses the strategies that supervisors can utilize to promote agency and ownership of learning and professionalism in school contexts. We consider how supervisors can use reflection in teacher preparation while candidates are engaged in their field experiences. Finally, the chapter addresses the need for ongoing professional development of supervisors and the various models for support of supervisors that can further encourage development of and engagement in their own practice.

Understanding Adult Learners

Early career teacher mentors are often viewed as qualified for the role because they were effective as P–12 classroom teachers. Yet, being skilled in teaching children does not guarantee that one is knowledgeable about the needs of adult learners; too often it is assumed that one facilitates the other. While it is critical that university supervisors have extensive and applicable knowledge about teaching children, in order to be effective in facilitating the development of useful pedagogical skills in a mentee it is not the only knowledge necessary. This section explores the knowledge about adult learners as a unique stage in the learning continuum, and considers how university supervisors might best gain and utilize knowledge about adult learners to support professional growth for novice teachers.

Knowles (1972) developed a concept of andragogy (teaching adults) as opposed to pedagogy (teaching children), focusing primarily on the assumptions about the learning of children that had informed adult learning up to that point. He argued that there are four different assumptions that guide andragogy: "(1) Changes in self-concept; (2) The role of experience; (3) Readiness to learn; and (4) Orientation to learning" (pp. 34–35). A fifth assumption was added in 1984 focusing on the motivation to learn—for adults this is predominantly internal (Knowles, 1984).

Acknowledging the changes in self-concept focuses primarily on the realization that adults have completed their psychological development and have achieved a sense of themselves as self-directing adults who are capable of determining their path and the needs they have to make progress along that path (Knowles, 1972). Experience plays a crucial part in the learning of adults. They are capable of using the broad range of their experiences to inform current and future learning; they expect to learn more from experience than from traditional forms of learning. "To an adult, his experience is who he is" (p. 35), and denial of this experience invalidates the person rather than just the experience itself.

Knowles' (1972) concept of readiness to learn focuses intensely on the need to learn materials or skills because of a professional or personal role that requires such knowledge or practice. Recommendations for andragogy focus on ensuring that adult learners are faced with the challenges of practice and then given the necessary experience, knowledge, or content to prepare them to address those challenges. Such an approach relates to Knowles's orientation of learning assumption, in that the adult

28   *The University Supervisor and Teacher Mentor*

learning has an immediate need for problem-solving related to the desire for specific application of knowledge to a current situation. Motivation to learn to teach is enhanced in this context though clinical experiences that drive a need to learn (American Association of Colleges of Teacher Education, 2018) and facilitate the identification of authentic challenges of practice.

Knowles (1984) identified four principles for adult learning that focus on the development of practical experiences to foster proactive learning outcomes. These four align directly with the assumptions about adult learning and focus on (1) problem-solving; (2) incorporating experiences and (3) real-world need as the basis for learning; and (4) including the adults in the development and assessment of instructional experiences. All of these principles are directly relevant to the work of supervision. This view of andragogy clearly aligns to adult learning needs in teacher education. Adults who are pursuing teaching as a career, during teacher preparation or during the early years of a career, are certainly driven by a desire to act on problems of practice. The refrain of "How will I use this?" becomes irrelevant in teacher education settings when opportunities to experience and practice using the new knowledge are prevalent. Supervision and mentoring of teacher education candidates is intimately linked to Knowles's (1972) assumptions of andragogy in terms of what novice teachers need: opportunities to define for themselves the necessary areas for problem-solving and growth and the support to get through that process.

A view of effective supervisory practice is driven with attention to the needs of adult learners and is informed by a concept of experience as the focus of collaboration between the mentor and novice educator. As the teacher's needs drive the collaborative interaction toward improving practice, real-world problems and context-specific needs are the focus of the joint work done by the pair.

Traditional Forms of Supervision in Teacher Education

Teacher education supervision has an incomplete history when it comes to truly understanding the practical theory as enacted by supervisors working with novice teachers and teacher candidates. Research on supervision has never achieved extensive development in the teacher education literature. Further, supervision has a reputation as a low-status, peripheral occupation in colleges of teacher education (Slick, 1998), and as such not worthy of extensive research efforts. Despite the continued use of supervisory practices to support teacher candidates, at times over the last 50 years it was noticeably absent from the research, aside to occasionally debate whether the position was financially viable relative to the support offered. The perception was often conveyed that mentoring and feedback was really only provided by the classroom teacher mentor and the university supervisor was an unnecessary expense to get university paperwork completed (Bowman, 1979). Universities often felt that this work could just as easily be done by the classroom-based mentor, and that little instructional value was offered through the role of the university supervisor (Rodgers & Keil, 2007). Much of this may be due to the perception that student teachers were uncritical in their replication of practices of the classroom teacher and the belief that behaviorist models undergird supervisory practice (Bieler, 2010). Over time, enough research has been conducted that demonstrates the value of the supervisor, namely when the role is thoughtfully engaged and professionally valued as key to supporting mentee learning (Richardson-Koehler, 1988; Zimpher, DeVoss, & Nott, 1980). These studies analyzed several different approaches to supervision and identified areas where the supervisor is centrally engaged in supporting mentees in various ways, including clinical, horizontal, and developmental approaches to practice.

Clinical Supervision

One of the moves made to further validate the role of the supervisor mirrors much of what is happening in medical education today, as many stakeholders seek to align the clinical experiences of teacher candidates to the models used more commonly in medical education programs. The desire to push the dialogue around teacher preparation and format learning experiences toward clinical residency models has resonated with educators who seek understanding and validation of the complexity of educational professionals' lives. In this vein, the discipline of education has regularly sought insight from other fields of professional practice. The clinical supervision model utilized in mentoring of teacher candidates reflects a history of the use of clinical supervision of therapists, psychologists, and others from social work professional fields. This model has provided a language and a structure that has been productively utilized by teacher education for some time.

Clinical supervision in teacher education is intimately tied to the evolution of teacher supervision more generally. The common school movement in the 1800s pushed the development of general supervision practices for teachers out of the hands of the clergy and into roles that were newly created to support the burgeoning school population and rapid growth of schools across the country (Marzano, Frontier, & Livingston, 2011). Initially, school superintendents did the work of traveling among schools and inspecting instruction. As the population boomed, the work was gradually handed off to what became school-level principals. While the focus of supervision was originally on streamlining instruction through the scientific approach (Marzano et al., 2011), eventually the work shifted toward a focus on the teachers and learning more about their work to improve instruction through attention to classroom observation.

30   *The University Supervisor and Teacher Mentor*

This shift of focus laid the groundwork for the development and expansion of models of clinical supervision, often considered comparable to the work occurring in medical professions because of the focus on the interaction that takes place while analyzing the observation in the clinical site (Cogan, 1973). The intention of the clinical supervision model is to encourage a strong, dialogue-based relationship between mentor and mentee focusing on careful discussion and analysis of practice (Goldhammer, 1969). Goldhammer (1969) developed a five-stage model for supervision that featured reflective dialogue about observations of classroom practice—these five stages are likely familiar to anyone working in supervisory fields: phase 1, pre-observation conference; phase 2, classroom observation; phase 3, analysis; phase 4, supervision conference; and phase 5, analysis of the analysis. Over time, phases 3 and 5 were dropped from most common usages of the model as emphasis on the best practices of teaching were defined through Madeline Hunter's model. The ongoing work of teacher evaluation evolved and narrowed (Marzano et al., 2011), costing the field much of "Goldhammer's vision of supervision as a collegial, inquiry-driven quest for more effective instructional practices" (p. 19).

However, in the 1980s the focus on the nuances of clinical supervision resurfaced with attention to more explicit work on reflective practices and developmental approaches (discussed further in the following section). Reflective models encouraged teachers to be invested and involved in the process, moving away from prescriptive views of supervision and evaluation that put all teachers through the same process (Glatthorn, 1984). Supervisory options were differentiated for experience, for need, and for the career goals of the teacher (Glatthorn, 1984; Glickman, 1985; McGreal, 1983).

This evolution of clinical supervision away from prescriptive models and back toward inquiry-driven reflective practice has resulted in the use of clinical supervision to drive the assumption that "Teachers are the agents of change in the instructional process in the public schools. If there is to be real improvement in the teacher's intellectual and behavioral skills, this change much occur at the site of instruction" (Hopkins & Moore, 1993, p. 77). With this vision in mind, mentors possess a great deal of power to help teacher candidates and novice teachers shape their views of effective practice and contribute to the development of teaching and learning. Encouraging novice teachers to adopt these views and practices moves schools toward environments that are equity-driven and responsive to student learning needs. This view of supervision facilitates supervisor agency through structuring experiences and systems of practice that provide generative opportunities for teacher reflection.

Horizontal Supervision

Horizontal supervision emerged in response to a trend in the early 1980s that attempted to reduce teaching to a series of competencies or skills

The University Supervisor and Teacher Mentor   31

that could be identified in practice and then taught, observed in clinical experiences, and mastered as a part of teacher education programs (Gitlin, 1981). Instead, horizontal supervision aimed "to expand the scope of evaluation so that theory is linked to practice and the goals of educational practice become a central focus of the supervision process" (Gitlin, 1981, p. 47). Helping candidates to reflect on the congruence of their intent and their realized practice is central to the role of the supervisor. Engaging in mentoring practice through this framework allows supervisors to support candidates in finding personal and powerful ways to engage classroom and school improvement. Above all, the supervisor plays a crucial role in helping the candidate interrogate the assumptions that underlie both intents and practices—the goal is not simply to replicate based on what was easy or worked, but rather to ensure that candidate goals are met through pedagogical practice and that the outcomes honor the rights and needs of the P–12 students. Supervisors' agency is utilized to ensure effective communication strategies are in place to support educators in this complex load by identifying areas of congruence and areas of disconnect and working to identify the strategies that can bring alignment between intent and practice.

Developmental Supervision

At the same time horizontal supervision was developed and described, there were several different models of developmental supervision in use that focused on the growth of the candidate over time and varied in the degree of clinical supervision strategies that were used in practice (Cohn & Gellman, 1988; Glickman, 1981, 1985; Glickman & Gordon, 1987). While some of these models clearly overlap in areas, unique contributions can come from each professional style of practice.

In the late 1970s and 1980s, Cohn and Gellman (1988) worked to design a supervision model that they felt supported the development of the teacher candidate across a semester-long student teaching experience. They sought to implement specific connections between the work happening in the university courses and the supervision that was provided in the field. Described as developmentally appropriate, they sought to utilize a series of different strategies to engage supervisors with candidates along their position on the developmental continuum. By focusing on the readiness of each candidate, the supervisor utilizes strategies that support the candidate with information she is ready to learn and frames approaches that encourage growth and also fosters reflection. The five models they used over the course of a student teaching semester included ego counseling, "first aid," "situational teaching," clinical practice, and group practice (p. 7). Situational teaching, in particular, invites the university supervisor into the conversation about best practices for educating candidates by inquiring and problem-solving together about the challenges of the classroom. "The role of the supervisor is akin to that of

32 *The University Supervisor and Teacher Mentor*

a teacher, asking probing questions to encourage students to see relationships, generate alternatives, and draw conclusions" (Cohn & Gellman, 1988, p. 4). Situational teaching:

> is directly tied to a particular curriculum, and its primary purpose is either to re-teach course concepts within the classroom situation or to generate alternative ways of looking at and handling classroom situations based upon previously taught curricular and analytical processes. This link to an explicit and shared curriculum intensifies the supervisory impact.
>
> (Cohn & Gellman, 1988, p. 7)

Developmental approaches share common practices with clinical supervision, but the nuances are ones that have the potential to engage supervisors in active opportunities to shape conversations about areas of challenge and to act on behalf of marginalized populations in educational settings. Providing supervisors agency can fully engage mentors as active members of powerful teacher education field experiences or early career classroom practices.

Early Career Mentoring Models

Two mentoring models receive repeated attention in the literature about mentoring early career teachers (Richter et al., 2013). The first is the work by Cochran-Smith and Paris (1995) that addresses whether mentoring offered to teachers is predicated on knowledge transmission or knowledge transformation. The second model, developed by Feiman-Nemser (2001), is founded on a vision of educative mentoring as compared to conventional mentoring. Both of these models emphasize the nature of the knowledge involved in learning—not simply a "sit and get" model of learning, but rather a constructivist approach that emphasizes knowing as an active process that drives learning, often through social interaction. Educative mentoring and knowledge transformation, the two more complex mentoring models, both function as approaches to teacher learning that encourage inquiry, exploration of teachers' questions, and the evolution of practice through continued learning. This contrasts with conventional mentoring and knowledge transmission, which focus much more on the technical aspects of orienting to the job (e.g., how to request copies or schedule conferences) and the basics of emotional support.

Mentors who engage in educative mentoring/knowledge transformation are focused on the ongoing learning and professional growth of the teacher as one with agency to enact change and create reflective responses to classroom activities. This vision of mentoring aligns to the notions of supervisors and mentors as active, contributing partners in making sense of teaching practice and building instructional growth—for teachers

The University Supervisor and Teacher Mentor 33

and students. This type of mentor agency has the power to influence the ongoing learning of the teacher and, as a result, the P–12 students in the teacher's care.

Common Strategies for Supervisory Practice

Research conducted over the past 40 years has identified some common practices that are used for mentoring of teacher education candidates and early career teachers. These include classroom observations of practice, review of lesson plans and associated materials, completion of rubrics or other scoring protocols to support observations (Slick, 1997), reflective journals, and pre- and post-observation conferences between mentor and mentee (sometimes including the classroom teacher) (Burns, Jacobs, & Yendol-Hoppey, 2016; Steadman, 2009). Additionally, many supervisors are required to meet with their mentees at several points during a clinical experience (or over the course of a school year for an early career teacher) for regular evaluation conferences to ensure acceptable development of skills and knowledge. As the increasing requirements for accountability, as described in Chapter 1, continue to inform teacher education practices, even more comprehensive evaluation processes and forms are developed that align expectations to national and discipline-specific standards for practice. In many cases, these forms come to consume much of the time supervisors spend on their role and in interactions with the mentees. However, effective supervision relies on a relationship that fosters interaction and exploration about teaching and not solely on the evaluative effects and outcomes of practice. While a number of models exist to support supervisors in developing and defining processes and boundaries of practice, less research looks at the specific skills that are needed to be an effective supervisor. Supervisors must possess pedagogical skills that support them in helping to break down the complexity of teaching for novices (Burns & Badiali, 2016). This section explores some prevailing strategies for supervisory practice and the consequences, both positive and negative, of these actions.

Pedagogical Skills

It is common to assume that because one has been a classroom teacher or administrator in a school, that the skills for supervision are present. Yet we acknowledge that the needs of adult learners are not typically addressed through teacher preparation for working with children. As such, most mentors lack professional expertise in working with or teaching adult learners. Thus, the pedagogical skills of supervisors or mentors must be developed and acknowledged, as a crucial part of an informed supervisory practice—teaching about teaching is not a simple process. Burns and Badiali (2016) identified six pedagogical skills that inform the work

34 *The University Supervisor and Teacher Mentor*

of supervisors: "(1) noticing, (2) ignoring, (3) intervening, (4) pointing, (5) unpacking, and (6) processing" (p. 162). These six together comprise a clinical pedagogy that can inform our understanding of the complexity of supervision. Developing this skill set in supervisors requires professional development that empowers supervisors to understand their own practice, to reflect on effective and ineffective moves with candidates, and to continually refine those skills through practice. Currently, there is an inaccurate assumption by teacher education programs and districts that the pedagogical skills of supervisors are in place because of previous teaching experience. Rather, professional development of supervisors is an area for growth in empowering supervisor and mentors to engage more intentionally in the refinement and development of their own skills. Promoting this sense of agency fosters a commitment to improving practice and ensuring that mentors are able to offer sophisticated learning experiences to mentees that build on their needs and respond to their ongoing growth and development as teachers.

Content Knowledge

Pedagogical skills for supervisors are crucial to practice but it is also necessary to focus on content knowledge and supervision that supports discipline-specific practices on the part of novices (Burbank, Bates, & Gupta, 2016). Focusing on one over the other—content knowledge versus pedagogical knowledge—is a losing proposition for teacher education (Burbank et al., 2012) because it implies that learning to teach can start in one knowledge base in isolation of the other. Teacher education must utilize an approach to content area supervision that privileges the pedagogical knowledge of how to engage the novice educator with strategies and understanding for how to take content-rich learning and ensure that it is accessible to P–12 students. Supervision that addresses the translation of content knowledge into quality pedagogy for students is a key step in moving teacher thinking beyond basic skills (Grossman, 2008). These challenges are particularly salient for secondary educators and supervisors where disciplinary organization of curriculum and instruction drives much of the daily lives of school communities.

A commitment to equity on the part of a supervisor necessitates attention to content area conventions that privilege and marginalize students, to pedagogy that invites students into their learning, and to awareness of the social and political climate of the school. Supervision that balances the tension of these sometimes competing forces is crucial to the success of quality instruction that meets multiple goals. Supervisors are invaluable to student teachers in supporting the navigation of the tensions between theory and practice—and with time, student teachers identify the need for explicit support in understanding the needs of diverse student populations in ways that facilitate content area learning (Burbank et al., 2016).

The University Supervisor and Teacher Mentor 35

This type of supervision empowers the mentor to help candidates realize the complexity of the professional knowledge base of teaching—to realize the power of merging the understanding of content with the supports for student learning that bring classroom success. Empowering mentors' agency to encourage this type of teacher agency is the kind of change that has a lasting impact on educational settings. Issues of equity and content knowledge as related to supervision will be taken up further in Chapter 3.

Dialogue and Questioning

Throughout all views of supervision that validate the consequences of an individual teacher's engagement in the process, dialogue plays a central role in the work. There is no meaningful engagement in the mentee's learning that is contextually situated without considering the role of discussion as a mediating factor in teacher development. The supervisor plays a powerful role in ensuring that this work is meaningful for learning and nuanced for the individual. Supervisors play a reconciling role in the process of making meaning from the university learning of the novice teacher as it comes to fruition in the field (Newell & Connors, 2011). According to Newell and Connors (2011), "Social and cultural factors mediate both teachers' and supervisors' development in particular contexts, and these settings are particularly powerful factors in shaping how participants envision their own practice and beliefs" (p. 227). Supervisors engage in feedback and dialogue that supports novice teachers' understanding of the ways that their beliefs are realized in practice. As a relative outsider to the cooperating teacher and student teacher relationship, supervisors are in a unique position to actively challenge and deconstruct experience with useful critical feedback about practice (Zimpher et al., 1980). When there are discordant elements to this realization, supervisors can use the power of these discussions to help candidates makes sense of what they see or hear and, from the discord, learn how to bring congruence to their work.

A key focus of this work is the role of questioning in dialogue. Nystrand (1997) determined that authentic questions (those that do not assume an answer) can support learners to challenge their own assumptions and identify the consequences of their ideas in action. Supervisory questioning that can foster this sort of growth is the type of mentoring work that utilizes supervision practices to enact change and growth in the classroom setting. Newell and Connors (2011) found that post-observation debriefings allowed the university supervisor to facilitate the type of dialogue and questioning that supported the teacher candidate. They reported that the teacher candidates were able to develop their understanding of how the skills and knowledge from teacher education programs were realized in their practice in the field, moving from shallow to deeper conceptual understanding of the various approaches being used with students.

36   *The University Supervisor and Teacher Mentor*

Supervisors become facilitators of educative mentoring practices that center on cognitive development (Achinstein & Athanases, 2006). Using conversation and dialogue to promote collaborative thinking is another way that the supervisor uses discussion to propel the novice forward as they "critically 'reframe' their thinking about students and classroom challenges, looking through new lenses and reconsidering their own practices and assumptions" (Achinstein & Athanases, 2006, p. 9). Key to this conceptualization about the value of the conversation is the impact it can also have on the supervisor, developing their skill set for future interactions while reflecting on their own practices. "Dialogic praxis in mentoring relationships can provide an important space for both mentor and student teacher to imagine and rehearse agentive action in contexts outside the mentoring relationship" (Bieler, 2010, p. 421). Utilizing these conversations between mentor and mentee can foster meaning-making that extends into daily classroom life (Bieler, 2010), supporting the agency of the teacher, and continuing to define the role of the supervisor as one with agency but also as one who encourages the development and active agency of novices.

Promoting Agency and Ownership

Supervisors are in the unique position of being both insider and outsider in that they have a relationship with the mentee but often not much more of a relationship with the children or the school setting, particularly outside of the presence of the mentee. This affords them the space and professional responsibility to support the children by focusing on the mentee and their work as a teacher. When positioned in this type of suspended space, there is much that a supervisor can do to facilitate the growth of a teacher. This collaborative mentoring practice is most effective when supervisors maintain the view of the teacher as someone who has the agency, the power, and responsibility to own and grow their professional practice. As early career teachers, many are simply focused on surviving the day, the week, the semester, and the year. It is a daunting task to engage in the day-to-day of teaching for the first time. Supervisors are a critical support for ensuring that the teacher is engaged both practically and theoretically.

While much has been written about the teacher burnout rate—41% of teachers leave the profession in the first 5 years (Ingersoll, Merrill, & Stuckey, 2014)—one of the prevailing solutions for addressing this rate has included increased support for educators in the form of mentors. Funding and strategies for consistently providing this support are wildly uneven among locales and are not sustained at the necessary rates. However, the mentoring work that has been done shows the power of an engaged support system to make a difference for early career teachers and their retention rate in the profession. There is much to be said of the opportunity to get this experience early in a career and work to encourage an attitude of agency and ownership for the profession that can empower each early career teacher. Supervisors are in the perfect position for this agency-building work with their commitments to the development of each mentee. Focusing directly on the growth and development of the teacher rather than on the outcomes and performance of each P–12 student means that supervisors are particularly well-suited to foster agency and to serve as guides as teachers embrace their agency and ownership for educational practices.

Purpose and Promotion of Reflection in Teacher Preparation

One of the most powerful ways for a supervisor to engage a mentee in the type of professional ownership and agency described in the previous section is through reflection in and on practice (Schon, 1983). Reflection *on action* is that which occurs after the teaching moment is over—as the candidate reflects on what worked and what did not during a given lesson or educational experience. Reflection *in action* is that which occurs in the moment—when the teacher is reflecting on and adjusting aspects of practice as it unfolds.

Reflection is a critical skill in education; it forces the teacher to confront the powerful realities of what occurs in the classroom each day (Burbank, Ramirez, & Bates, 2012). However, it is exactly the intensity of the classroom reality that reinforces the challenge of engaging in reflection—when does one have time and how does one learn to reflect with purpose and intention? Surely some of the reflection of the classroom experience is in pursuit of efficiency, but the powerful reflection that occurs around an educator's commitments to practice, the intentions of instruction, and the success in meeting student needs is crucial to growth and development. Identifying the most effective strategies for an individual supervisor's role in this work is crucial for ensuring that each paired relationship is educative for both partners. A supervisor's stance towards reflective practice as a central part of agency impacts the outcomes for teacher candidates and novice teachers.

There are a number of ways that supervisors are both involved and responsible for fostering a climate of reflection as an essential part of learning to teach. Research has shown that supervisors are critical to the development of reflective habits in teacher candidates (Bates et al., 2011; Nguyen, 2009). Educative mentoring (Feiman-Nemser, 2001) or a knowledge-transformation (Cochran-Smith & Paris, 1995) approach to mentoring requires concentrated attention to reflection. Reflection has taken root as a critical part of the teacher education curriculum, but the

38 *The University Supervisor and Teacher Mentor*

linkages must be explicit and intentional for candidates to understand and appreciate the purpose of the reflective process:

> Powerful teacher education programs have a clinical curriculum as well as a didactic curriculum. They teach candidates to turn analysis into action by applying what they are learning in curriculum plans, teaching applications, and other performance assessments that are organized on professional teaching standards. These attempts are especially educative when they are followed by systematic reflection on student learning in relation to teaching and receive detailed feedback, with opportunities to retry and improve.
>
> (Darling-Hammond, 2006, p. 308)

When educators are able to make these connections clear, and help mentees see the value of the reflection in challenging assumptions about practice and ensuring that continued improvement to practice can happen, supervisors have the space to address and pursue change at the individual, classroom, school, and system levels.

Models for Support of Supervisors

There is a crucial gap that is unfilled for university supervisors. Typically, they work in isolation from others doing the same type of work and lack the support of a professional community for collaboration and discussion (Snyder & D'Emidio-Caston, 2001). They are assigned one-to-one with students, and if a supervisor supervises more than one candidate, they typically work as a mentee group in a seminar or professional development format. While there is certainly value in supporting candidates with seminar sessions together, where brainstorming, idea development, and problem-solving can occur with a supportive group of peers, the same type of support is rarely offered to supervisors.

Mentors for early career teachers are sometimes afforded more support for their work through mentoring programs that are funded by a grant or district/state that incorporate additional training and sharing opportunities for mentors. But, by and large, many mentors find themselves in the same boat as supervisors who struggle to find like-minded peers who are working through the same challenges as they engage in practice in the field.

However, there are models that potentially alleviate this isolation and foster the types of professional development that encourage the continued development of mentoring/coaching and supervising practices that benefit teachers. These include professional learning communities (PLCs) (DuFour, 2004), commonly used in teaching settings that foster data analysis and refinement of practice. There is also potential for the use of book clubs and critical friends to support growth of practice. This section will address the potential of these models to foster a collaborative and supportive community for those engaged in mentoring and coaching practices.

Professional Learning Communities

Professional development (PD) has a reputation as a means for implementing top-down mandates and quickly shifting priorities (Hargreaves, 2000; Lieberman, 1995; Sandholtz, 1999) where teachers often feel that they barely get a handle on the new program or focus of the district before it has been shelved and they are off to the next mandated PD session. Professional learning communities (PLCs) are an increasingly common form of professional development located onsite in the school and situated in teachers' daily classroom practices. The PLC structure incorporates many of the assumptions of andragogy described earlier in the chapter and are particularly well-suited to supporting adult learners. As discussed in Chapter 5, PLCs serve as an opportunity to develop educators' leadership and mentoring potential. Situated cognition is learning in a social context (Lave & Wenger, 1991) which correlates well to the work of school communities. Much of what is learned while on the job is gleaned from the local community—colleagues and others in the professional setting (Lave & Wenger, 1991)—and is referred to as a "community of practice." For teaching PLCs to be successful and truly collaborative, the focus must be on instructional practices (DuFour, 2004). While there are other ways that teachers can collaborate or that professional development can be administered to enhance the profession, to have a true impact on what occurs in the classroom the collaboration of teachers must center on instruction. According to Smith (2011), "Evidence is building that change in instructive practice does not occur unless faculty become involved in leadership, including professional development and professional learning communities" (p. 1).

PLCs have the potential to empower the mentor/supervisor through collaboration around mentoring practice. Developing structures that support professional development for supervisors has long been a challenge for universities and districts. Logistics of time, distance among supervisors and school sites, reimbursement for additional work, and structures for support that still empower the mentors have complicated the implementation of models that foster this type of focused collaboration. "Working in a supportive, professional community that valued their own thinking and reflective practice" (Owens, 2010, p. 51) supported teachers in developing a system for their classroom that honored these same values for their students. Creating this type of system for teacher mentors and supervisors is worth the effort for the potential it has to encourage reflection on and investment in mentoring practices. Communities "assume a focus on shared purpose, mutual regard and caring, and

40   *The University Supervisor and Teacher Mentor*

an insistence on integrity and truthfulness" (Lambert, 2003, p. 4). While learning the collaborative norms of the group can be challenging at the beginning (Spencer, 2016), and developing practices that foster transparent, open sharing of practice can be personally exposing, the work that can come of this to improve practice is worth the discomfort.

Book Clubs

At times, PLCs may need a place to start—to work together to develop a sense of community and collaboration around less personally revealing content than the examination of practice. This may be particularly true for mentors or university supervisors who work in diverse settings and do not share a school or office space, but work one-on-one with mentees in relative isolation from each other. At these times, starting with an ongoing discussion about a piece of literature or a professional text can provide some common ground for beginning to explore beliefs, values, and commitment of practice (Burbank, Kauchak, & Bates, 2010).

Book clubs can provide mentors with the opportunities to explore best practices and personal beliefs by reading about others' perspectives (George, 2002). While professional book clubs may not be frequently offered to practicing teachers (Commeyras & DeGroof, 1998), the opportunities to build understanding, explore diverse perspectives about mentoring practices and associated issues, and grapple with complex issues of teacher education suggest that book clubs can be a powerful entry into a more engaged professional practice (Burbank et al., 2010). Research (Burbank et al., 2010) suggests that book club conversations have the potential to spill over into other areas of practice—fostering conversation with colleagues and mentors that do not participate in the book club. Further, book clubs can foster potential for continued collaboration among mentors that arise from opportunities to learn more about each other and share practice. They also can facilitate ongoing learning through powerful models such as critical friends.

Critical Friends

A critical friend "is a trusted person who asks provocative questions, provides data to be examined through another lens, and offers critique of a person's work as a friend" (Costa & Kallick, 1993, p. 50). Critical friends groups (currently supported by the National School Reform Faculty, n.d.) are often used as a source of professional development interaction and strong observational feedback for school improvement processes (Bambino, 2002; Curry, 2008; Dunne, Nave, & Lewis, 2000). The intention of these groups is to empower teachers to act as agents and managers of their own learning—a type of practitioner inquiry (Dunne & Honts, 1998; Franzak, 2002) that is not always offered to teachers in a top-down administrative structure that is often used to select, assign, or implement professional development in schools. Additionally, it is a model that can be used to facilitate students of all ages (P–12 and university) in the writing process (Costa & Kallick, 1993; Dunne et al., 2000), support student teachers in coming to know themselves as teachers (Franzak, 2002), and encourage reflective practice in teachers (Dunne & Honts, 1998). The outcome of this work can shift teachers' roles from reinforcing the status quo to becoming agents of change, able and willing to be collegial and transparent about their work and their students' learning (Norman, Golian, & Hooker, 2005).

Critical friends groups typically incorporate protocols where teachers bring samples of student work or teaching artifacts (lesson plans, handouts, etc.) to the meeting, share insights and questions with colleagues, and then work together on observational feedback designed not to judge but to support the teacher in making sense of next steps for student learning or teaching practice. The work of critical friends can support all sorts of professional learning opportunities, as well as supervisors and mentors of candidates and classroom teachers. The structure of ongoing professional development and intentional, focused learning about practice is not commonly offered to mentors. However, the critical friends model provides a method for encouraging supervisors to open up about practice and share innovations, struggles, and student needs.

The transparency of practice that results from this type of shared observation and support changes the nature and flow of feedback. Teachers often comment on the relative isolation of life in the classroom—in the way of access to other adults to foster conversation, to encourage sharing of classroom challenges—and this separation can be even more prevalent for supervisors or mentors. One-to-one relationships between mentors and candidates are intense and typically result in inviting few or no others into the interaction. Determining how best to respond to a candidate's needs is usually fairly independent work and can be very isolating if few others are familiar with the person, context, or relationship. Developing communities of mentoring critical friends where supervisors can work together to find ongoing understanding about the individual inquiries that each supervisor is pursuing to support their candidates can foster observational reflection on practice. "CFGs promote an inquiry-oriented, practice-based, self-disclosing form of conversation that creates opportunities for teachers to raise questions about and carefully examine their practice and students' learning" (Lord, 1994, cited in Norman, Golian, & Hooker, 2005, p. 285). This vision of critical friends proposes a view of learning about practice that benefits the mentor as well as the mentee in terms of the new insights and options that the mentor brings to each interaction. Two components are explored through this approach that push the mentoring practice forward: (1) thoughtful and purposeful questioning of practice—what is seen, what it means, where there are

42 *The University Supervisor and Teacher Mentor*

areas for growth—and (2) reflection that fosters deeper understanding of the nuances of practice—how to truly use supervisory moves to help a teacher grow in the most meaningful ways.

When considering the outcomes of practice as a means of transforming supervisory practice, critical friends can serve a central role for self-study (Loughran & Northfield, 1996). Self-study of practice encourages careful and explicit attention to the work of studying one's own practice— identifying areas of success or strength and areas for growth. However, one of the challenges with self-study centers on ensuring that the data and analysis does not become uncritically self-affirming (Russell & Schuck, 2004). Improving practice through self-study focuses on careful consideration of ways that one can support self and others in making judgments and decisions about reflections on practice, studying carefully how the implementation of practice informs learning. In this case, critical friends play a powerful role as a sounding board, reflecting back what is heard in constructive and collegial ways but that also ensure the intent to challenge the supervisor to reflect on and improve practice. Doing so provides the supports necessary for the mentor to improve practice, to own the process of learning, and to grow as a supervisor with the power to impact the practice of so many early career teachers.

Conclusion

Adult learners are a unique population and supervision has evolved in response to the learning needs that are represented in experiential, clinical-based models of practice. When assumptions and principles of andragogy guide the development of experiences and the formats of supervision that are utilized to support adult learners, the potential exists to create rich learning opportunities for the novice educators and also for the mentors who support them. An overwhelming issue in the practice of teacher mentors is the little support or guidance offered to them beyond describing, defining, and processing the functional responsibilities of the role. Identifying specific experiences that can be offered in support of mentors is a critical area for growth of this profession to benefit all.

Research has shown that early career support is crucial in ensuring that teachers stay in the profession. Empowering mentors to fully engage their role in this interaction can ameliorate the number of teachers exiting the profession. Strategies shared in this chapter can reshape the professional lives of mentors to more fully support their growth and development as leaders and agents of change that impact the lives of early career teachers. Mentors who are active, engaged, and feel the agency to empower teachers to create climates in schools that are supportive of learning for new teachers are precisely the force needed in teacher education programs and districts across the country.

References

Achinstein, B., & Athanases, S. (Eds.). (2006). *Mentors in the making: Developing new leaders for new teachers*. New York, NY: Teachers College Press.

American Association of Colleges of Teacher Education. (2018). *A pivot toward clinical practice, its lexicon, and the renewal of educator preparation*. Washington, DC: Author.

Bambino, D. (2002). Critical friends. *Educational Leadership, 56*(6), 25–27.

Bates, A. J., Drits, D., & Ramirez, L. A. (2011). Self-awareness and enactment of supervisory stance: Influences on responsiveness toward student teacher learning. *Teacher Education Quarterly, 38*(3), 69–87.

Bieler, D. (2010). Dialogic praxis in teacher preparation: A discourse analysis of mentoring talk. *English Education, 42*(4), 391–426.

Bowman, N. (1979). College supervision of student teaching: A time to reconsider. *Journal of Teacher Education, 30*(3), 29–30.

Burbank, M. D., Bates, A. J., & Gupta, U. (2016). The influence of teacher development on secondary content area supervision among preservice teachers. *The Teacher Educator, 51*(1), 55–69.

Burbank, M. D., Kauchak, D., & Bates, A. J. (2010). Book study groups as professional development opportunities for preservice and practicing teachers: An exploratory study. *The New Educator, 6*(1), 56–73. doi:10.1080/15476 88X.2010.10399588

Burbank, M. D., Ramirez, L., & Bates, A. J. (2012). Critically reflective thinking in urban teacher education: A comparative case study of two participants' experiences as content specialists. *The Professional Educator, 36*(2).

Burns, R. W., & Badiali, B. (2016). Unearthing the complexities of clinical pedagogy in supervision: Identifying the pedagogical skills of supervisors. *Action in Teacher Education, 38*(2), 156–174. doi:10.1080/01626620.2016.1155097

Burns, R. W., Jacobs, J., & Yendol-Hoppey, D. (2016). The changing nature of the role of the university supervisor and function of preservice teacher supervision in an era of clinically-rich practice. *Action in Teacher Education, 38*(4), 410–425. doi:10.1080/01626620.2016.1226203

Cochran-Smith, M., & Paris, C. L. (1995). Mentor and mentoring: Did Homer have it right? In J. Smyth (Ed.), *Critical discourses on teacher development* (pp. 181–202). London: Cassell.

Cogan, M. L. (1973). *Clinical supervision*. Boston, MA: Houghton Mifflin Harcourt.

Cohn, M. M., & Gellman, V. C. (1988). Supervision: A developmental approach for fostering inquiry in preservice teacher education. *Journal of Teacher Education, 39*(2), 2–8.

Commeyras, M., & DeGroof, L. (1998). Literacy professionals' perspectives on professional development and pedagogy: A United States survey. *Reading Research Quarterly, 33*(4), 434–472.

Costa, A. L., & Kallick, B. (1993). Through the lens of a critical friend. *Educational Leadership, 51*(2), 49–51.

Curry, M. (2008). Critical friends groups: The possibilities and limitations embedded in teacher professional communities aimed at instructional improvement and school reform. *Teachers College Record, 110*(4), 733–774.

44 The University Supervisor and Teacher Mentor

Darling-Hammond, L. (2006). Constructing 21st century teacher education. *Journal of Teacher Education*, *57*(3), 300–314. doi:10.1177/0022487105285962

DuFour, R. (2004). What is a professional learning community? *Educational Leadership*, *61*(8), 6–11.

Dunne, F., & Honts, F. (1998, April). *"That group really makes me think!" Critical friends groups and the development of reflective practitioners*. Paper presented at the American Educational Research Association annual conference, San Diego, CA.

Dunne, F., Nave, B., & Lewis, A. (2000, December). Critical friends groups: Teachers helping teachers improve student learning. *Phi Delta Kappa Research Bulletin*, *28*, 9–12.

Feiman-Nemser, S. (2001). Helping novices learn to teach: Lessons from an exemplary support teacher. *Journal of Teacher Education*, *52*(1), 17–30.

Franzak, J. (2002). Developing a teacher identity: The impact of Critical Friends Practice on the student teacher. *English Education*, *34*(4), 258–280.

George, M. (2002). Professional development for a literature-based middle school curriculum. *The Clearing House*, *75*(6), 327–331.

Gitlin, A. (1981). Horizontal supervision: An approach to student teacher supervision. *Journal of Teacher Education*, *32*(5), 47–50.

Gimbert, B., & Nolan, J. F. (2003). The influence of professional development school context on supervisory practice: A university supervisor's and interns' perspectives. *Journal of Curriculum and Supervision*, *18*(4), 353–379.

Glatthorn, A. A. (1984). *Differentiated supervision*. Alexandria, VA: Association for Supervision and Curriculum Development.

Glickman, C. D. (1981). *Developmental supervision: Alternative approaches for helping teachers improve instruction*. Alexandria, VA: Association for Supervision and Curriculum Development.

Glickman, C. D. (1985). *Supervision of instruction: A developmental approach*. Boston, MA: Allyn & Bacon.

Glickman, C. D., & Gordon, S. P. (1987). Chancing developmental supervision. *Educational Leadership*, *44*(8), 64–68.

Goldhammer, R. (1969). *Clinical supervision: Special methods for supervision of teachers*. New York, NY: Holt, Rinehart, and Winston.

Grossman, P. (2008). Teaching development: Experience and philosophy (using the three Rs). *Teacher Education Quarterly*, *35*(2), 155–163.

Hargreaves, A. (2000). *Changing teachers, changing times: Teachers' work and culture in the postmodern age*. London: Continuum International Publishing Group.

Hopkins, W. S., & Moore, K. D. (1993). *Clinical supervision: A practical guide to student teacher supervision*. Madison, WI: Brown & Benchmark Publishers.

Ingersoll, R., Merrill, L., & Stuckey, D. (2014). *Seven trends: The transformation of the teaching force*. Report prepared by The Consortium for Policy Research in Education, Philadelphia, PA.

Knowles, M. S. (1972). Innovations in teaching styles and approaches based upon adult learning. *Journal of Education for Social Work*, *8*(2), 32–30.

Knowles, M. S. (1984). *Andragogy in action*. San Francisco, CA: Jossey-Bass.

Lambert, L. (2003). *Leadership capacity for lasting school improvement*. Alexandria, VA: Association for Supervision and Curriculum Development.

Lave, J., & Wenger, E. (1991). *Situated learning: Legitimate peripheral participation*. Cambridge: Cambridge University Press.

Lee, Y. A. (2011). Self-study of cross-cultural supervision of teacher candidates for social justice. *Studying Teacher Education, 7*(1), 2–18.

Lieberman, A. (1995). Practices that support teacher development: Transforming conceptions of professional learning. *Phi Delta Kappan, 76*(8), 591–596.

Loughran, J., & Northfield, J. (1996). *Opening the classroom door: Teacher, researcher, learner*. London: Falmer Press.

Marzano, R. J., Frontier, T., & Livingston, D. (2011). *Effective supervision: Supporting the art and science of teaching*. Alexandria, VA: Association for Supervision and Curriculum Development.

McGreal, T. (1983). *Successful teacher evaluation*. Alexandria, VA: Association for Supervision and Curriculum Development.

National School Reform Faculty. (n.d.). *Critical friends groups*. Retrieved from www.nsrfharmony.org

Newell, G., & Connors, S. (2011). "Why do you think that?" A supervisor's mediation of a preservice English teacher's understanding of instructional scaffolding. *English Education, 43*(3), 225–261.

Nguyen, H. T. (2009). An inquiry-based practicum model: What knowledge, practices, and relationships typify empowering teaching and learning experiences for student teachers, cooperating teachers, and college supervisors? *Teaching & Teacher Education, 25*(5), 655–662. doi:10.1016/j.tate.2008.10.001

Norman, P. J., Golian, K., & Hooker, H. (2005). Professional development schools and Critical Friends Groups: Supporting student, novice and teacher learning. *The New Educator, 1*(4), 273–286. doi:10.1080/15476880500276793

Nystrand, M. (1997). *Opening dialogue: Understanding the dynamics of language and learning in the English classroom*. New York, NY: Teachers College Press.

Owens, R. (2010). New schools of thought: Developing thinking and learning communities. *International Journal of Learning, 17*(6), 43–54.

Richardson-Koehler, V. (1988, March–April). Barriers to the effective supervision of student teaching: A field study. *Journal of Teacher Education,* 28–34.

Richter, D., Kunter, M., Ludtke, O., Klusmann, U., Anders, Y., & Baumert, J. (2013). How different mentoring approaches affect beginning teachers' development in the first years of practice. *Teaching and Teacher Education, 36*, 166–177. http://dx.doi.org/10/1016/j.tate.2013.07.012

Rodgers, A., & Keil, V. L. (2007). Restructuring a transitional student teacher supervision model: Fostering enhanced professional development and mentoring within a professional development school context. *Teaching & Teacher Education, 23*(1), 63–80. doi:10.1016/j.tate.2006.04.012

Russell, T., & Schuck, S. (2004, June). How critical are critical friends and how critical should they be? In *The Fifth International Conference on Self-Study of Teacher Education Practices*.

Sandholtz, J. (1999). *A comparison of direct and indirect professional development activities*. Paper presented at the 1999 annual meeting of the American Educational Research Association, Montreal, Canada.

Schon, D. (1983). *The reflective practitioner: How professionals think in action*. New York, NY: Basic Books.

46 The University Supervisor and Teacher Mentor

Slick, S. K. (1997). Assessing versus assisting: The supervisor's role in the complex dynamic of the student teaching triad. *Teaching and Teacher Education*, *13*(7), 713–726.

Slick, S. K. (1998). The university supervisor: A disenfranchised outsider. *Teaching and Teacher Education*, *14*(8), 821–834.

Smith, S. (2011). Instructional designers as leaders in professional learning communities: Catalysts for transformative change. *Academic Leadership*, *9*(4), 1–11.

Snyder, J., & D'Emidio-Caston, M. (2001). Becoming a teacher of teachers: Two dilemmas in taking up preservice supervision. In F. O. Rust & R. Freidus (Eds.), *Guiding school change: The role of work of change agents* (pp. 102–120). New York, NY: Teachers College Press.

Spencer, E. J. (2016). Professional learning communities: Keeping the focus on instructional practice. *Kappa Delta Pi Record*, *52*(2), 83–85. doi:10.1080/002 28958.2016.1156544

Steadman, S. (2009). Cycles of confidence: Supporting university supervisors' recursive trajectories of development. *Teaching and Learning*, *23*(3), 98–110.

Zimpher, N. L., DeVoss, G., & Nott, D. (1980). A closer look at university student teacher supervision. *Journal of Teacher Education*, *31*(4), 11–15.

3 Supervision as an Informed Craft

Supervisory support is complex; it is more than simply implementing observation and evaluation protocols or teaching others technical skills (Slick, 1998a). Supervisors are encouraged to build a practice that includes "elements such as a focus on relationships and partnerships, research and innovation, curriculum, and individual [preservice student teacher] support" (Jacobs, Hogarty, & Burns, 2017, p. 176). Teacher education is a field where intentional efforts are put into program design, program goals, curriculum, etc., and yet these efforts are not realized in practice, partly because teacher education as intended is not always what is enacted (Zeichner & Tabachnick, 1982).

Supervisors work with student teachers to realize a program's goals and designs in action in classrooms. Whether this happens with fidelity to programming or with widely disparate experiences between candidates, the outcomes inform a great deal of the current understanding about realized practice. Recognizing the essential elements of the complex craft of supervision is key to building programs that can sustain translation into the enactment in the field. As knowledgeable mentors, supervisors utilize their professional and career background experiences, teaching beliefs, understanding of educational and classroom context, and more to inform their theoretical and philosophical stances as they guide pedagogical decisions (Bates, Drits, & Ramirez, 2011). Understanding these influences is particularly critical in the context of today's schools in terms of student diversity and the intensity of curricular and accountability emphases at the district, state, and national levels.

Teachers who have agency feel comfortable addressing classroom diversity through relationships with students and strong curriculum and classroom management, which can reduce teacher burnout; feelings of disempowerment result in teachers who leave the field (Miller & McIntyre, 2012) and agency can be one antidote to those feelings. Teacher education programs that use course experiences and critically reflective practices to develop educational equity encourage teachers to become responsible for their own agency (Flessner, Miller, Patrizio, & Horwitz, 2012). While teacher educators are increasingly committed

48   *Supervision as an Informed Craft*

to the work of identifying program-specific ways to build candidate knowledge bases, supervision is not addressed as intentionally or publicly as a part of the program's support structures for candidates. As introduced in Chapter 1, calls for social justice education, increasing awareness of the complexity of students' lives on the parts of teachers, and the need for equity in educational opportunity all require attention and support provided by supervisors to help teachers respond to these needs. Discussion of research from these areas will develop the notion of supervision as a culturally responsive act in today's classrooms, looking specifically at the agency required of supervisors. Supervisors act as agents of change when they engage this type of conversation and support for novice teachers. This modeling can propel teachers forward in developing their own socially just practices that shape the experiences of school-age children.

Particular attention in this chapter is directed at the context of supervision and the intersection of influences, such as teaching background, on the practice and agency of the supervisor. This chapter also examines the impact of content area disciplinary knowledge (e.g., math, foreign language, or science) and how content informs the type and form of supervision—both what is offered and what is deemed valuable by the novice teacher. Throughout this chapter, there will be an explicit focus on agency as a crucial part of supervisory practice with the intention of growing, developing, and enacting change as a pertinent responsibility of the supervisor in modeling best practices for growth with novice teachers.

Impact of Personal and Professional History on a Supervisor

In general, as described in Chapter 2, supervision of preservice teachers is an under-researched area of professional practice in teacher preparation. Yet, it is a complex practice that requires attention to the needs of teacher candidates, the context of schools, and the skills of effective relationship management (Jacobs et al., 2017). According to Zahorik (1988), a common approach to supervision "defies human nature" (p. 14), because it fails to acknowledge individuality and situation, and leaves us searching for context and broad strokes that do define the work. The research literature has insufficient insight into the work that goes on in the daily interactions of supervisors and preservice or early career teachers they mentor. As Clift and Brady (2005) reported, "The content and nature of supervisory conferences, the relations between feedback and subsequent performance, and the struggle among role groups are examples of research topics that seem to have been lost" (p. 329). Yet, other research over the past 30 years does show that the supervisor is an important player in the process of learning to teach (Bates et al., 2011; Friebus, 1977;

Grant & Zozakiewicz, 1995; Jacobs et al., 2017; Zimpher, DeVoss, & Nott, 1980).

Supervisors are tasked with the responsibility to bridge theory and practice by merging the university and school worlds through attention to the realization of coursework into teaching and learning experiences with students (Bates et al., 2011; Gimbert & Nolan, 2003). Supervisors are the primary support for the teacher candidate and must support and advocate for their learning, given that the primary responsibilities of the cooperating (classroom) teacher focus on the P–12 students (Slick, 1998a, 1998b). One strategy supervisors encourage their candidates to use is critical reflection (Jacobs et al., 2017) in the crucial analysis of practice that improves teacher competency and agency over time. When supervisors are viewed as a chief influence on the development of the candidate and a powerful messenger of the university's view of quality teaching and learning, there is potential for a great deal of impact on the future teaching practices of the candidate. As such, building supervisory practice from the previous experiences of classroom teaching—without much other guidance from which to build—means that the prior practice holds a magnified influence in the framing of their new work as a mentor.

As the teacher candidate is hired as a beginning teacher, mentors for early career teachers serve in a comparable role as university supervisors. Research on the role and responsibilities of the mentor is more comprehensive than that focused on university supervisors and indicates that the mentor can have a positive impact on the induction process of novice teachers. Mentors provide valuable insight into the practicalities of the teaching role (Lindgren, 2005), serve as a crucial support for the first year of teaching (Marable & Raimondi, 2007), and can result in improved instruction (Rozelle & Wilson, 2012; Stanulis & Floden, 2009). As such, how the supervisor or mentor views the world of education matters a great deal to the candidate or novice teacher, to the university or school district, and to the profession. This influential power can be instrumental in shaping the ongoing evolution of the novice teacher and, as such, not only the educator's influence on the students taught but on the schools more generally.

Recent research indicates that supervisors are chiefly tenured faculty and retired adjunct faculty (Jacobs et al., 2017) but little is known about the professional development that is offered to supervisors that addresses the unique nature of the role. Despite the findings of the research, many in the profession are often graduate students and retired teachers or school administrators; thus, it is difficult to know how much they understand about supervisory practices and conceptual understanding of mentoring adult learners (Jacobs et al., 2017). Greater understanding is needed about how the personal and professional backgrounds and experiences that the supervisor brings to the mentoring relationship affect practice and inform decision-making on a range of topics relevant to

50 Supervision as an Informed Craft

novice teacher support. Research by Bates et al. (2011) looks at how the supervisor's stance influences professional mentoring practices:

> A *stance* [emphasis in the original] is a supervisor's professional knowledge, perspective, and conceptualization about how student teachers learn to teach in the classroom context. Stances include issues such as how learner learn, what effective classroom instruction looks like, and how to prepare teachers to meet the needs of diverse learners.
>
> (Bates et al., 2011, p. 70)

The research indicates that supervisors pull from the range of their own personal and professional experiences as they develop the skills and toolkit they utilize in the role of supervisor. While P–12 teaching practice is certainly relevant here, and informs the professional understanding of learning and teaching that guides mentorship of novice educators, stance is a more nuanced perception of how these pieces come together to guide beliefs about working with novices. This may explain the supervisor's heavy reliance on previous experiences as a teacher and/or administrator to build the skill base and knowledge for supervision.

Several qualitative research studies have looked at the evolution of supervisors from graduate students to teacher educators; some focusing on the responsibilities in the role of university supervisor and how they came to understand that work (Bullock, 2012; Williams, Ritter, & Bullock, 2012). This research shows that the progress into understanding and learning the supervisory role is left in the hands of the graduate student. Relatively little mentoring or professional development is offered by programs or universities to support learning this new position. While the intentions on the part of the graduate students are usually positive, too many times that may mean that inconsistencies in experience have a significant impact on preservice teachers' experiences.

Yet, the field of teacher preparation has recognized for years that "Becoming a university supervisor '[involves] transformation, the construction of new knowledge, identities, ways of knowing, and new positionings of oneself in the world'" (Beach, 1999, p. 113, cited in Newell & Connors, 2011, p. 229). As such, innovative programs and universities are looking for ways to intentionally facilitate their supervisors' professional growth. While the notion of professional development for supervisors has come and gone over the years through the research (e.g., Zeichner & Liston, 1985), there are continued efforts, primarily local, to build these opportunities. For example, one program is requiring supervisors to take an on-campus supervision course with program leadership to learn more about the history, research, and best practices of supervision while employed by the university as a supervisor. Participant feedback indicates that this experience resulted in greater understanding of personal and professional beliefs about supervision and a deeper understanding of the history and development of supervisory practice (Bates & Burbank, 2018). The group's conversation that came from shared space and discussion around lived practice made a difference for participants resulting in a "level of collaboration—working and problem solving together—[that] was empowering" (Bates & Burbank, 2018). This type of interactive, theoretical learning while engaged in practical application in the field supports supervisors in the recursive cycle of engaging in, reflecting on, and improving practice to facilitate candidate learning.

The Impact of Supervisory Stance on How One Supervises

Supervisors engage with candidates through the lens of a particular stance toward their practice that is driven by their worldview and experiences as an educator in contexts other than the classroom (Bates et al., 2011). Research on supervisory practice indicates that previous professional development experiences directly impact the ways that supervisors choose to engage with their candidates, influencing which beliefs and actions get priority when working together. Stances can be impacted by the supervisor's self-awareness of the stance (Do I know and reflect on why I do what I do?). Secondly, stances are influenced by the nature of the personal and professional experiences that are informing supervisory practice, attending specifically to those that carry the most weight with the supervisor. Finally, stances are impacted by the degree of clarity with candidates about expectations regarding supervisor roles and practices, noticing how clearly these beliefs are communicated with student teachers. These three factors directly play into the degree of the interaction held around explicit mentoring of teacher candidates and can openly influence the outcomes of the experience.

Central to these three factors is supervisory self-awareness. The research conducted by Bates and colleagues (2011) details the unique nuances that denote varying degrees of reflection on practice. The researchers defined a complex stance as one that "recognizes and affirms the multilayered nature of teaching that challenges student teachers because of the many nuances that are relevant to the practice" (p. 75). By comparison, stances that are less complex will focus:

> more on the "here and now" of supervising and less on the eventual future and growth of the candidate as a teacher, often relying more on the logistics of what the supervisor sees and does as a part of her job than on teacher development.
>
> (p. 75)

52 *Supervision as an Informed Craft*

On the other hand, a complex stance is well positioned to ensure that the supervisor is enacting agency about the practice of becoming a teacher through the specific actions, attitudes, and the collaborative nature of the work. This can enhance educator agency development through engagement in complex practices from the earliest days of learning to teach. This connected form of agency and supervisory work can result in an educator's strong sense of self, which may also encourage resistance to burnout in the early years of a career. The distinction between more and less complex stances is obvious in that a more complex stance has the potential to have a far greater impact on the outcomes of the experience for both the supervisor and the student teacher.

Reflection on practice is key to this work. Opportunities to participate in collaborative reflection with other supervisors, by discussing student feedback and sharing best practices, are cited as key to the growth of supervisory stance over time (Bates et al., 2011). Note that stances are not linear; they evolve and change over time (Rust, 1988) in response to continued learning, ongoing experience, and the development of practice. Just as teachers do, supervisors change and evolve through reflection and opportunity. Given that "what is emphasized, and presumably learned, in a student teaching program is, in large part, a function of his or her relationship with a university supervisor" (Zahorik, 1988, p. 14), it is of fundamental importance that supervisors have support in ongoing reflection about practice—what is working, what is not, what should be changed and why, how student teachers are responding to various methods or strategies for mentoring, the challenges of schools and the concurrent needs of P–12 students, and so on. Sorting out how the supervisor impacts this work in meaningful ways that build agency is one significant way to ensure experiences of quality in the P–12 classroom.

Developing Triadic Relationships

Student teaching successes often hinge on the student teacher and cooperating teacher relationship (Beck & Kosnik, 2002). Research has shown the influence that the cooperating teacher's' beliefs have on the development of the student teacher's belief and practice (Bullock, 2012), regardless of how effective either is with teaching and learning (Rozelle & Wilson, 2012). Weiss and Weiss (2001) found that "cooperating teachers are the most powerful influence on the quality of the student teaching experience and often shape what student teachers learn by the way they mentor" (p. 134). The research in cooperating teacher and student teacher relationships focuses extensively on the power dynamic that is present in the relationship and the influence it can have on a student teacher's ability to respond to challenges they see in the classroom (Anderson, 2007; Glenn, 2006; Veal & Rikard, 1998). These power dynamics have an influence

Supervision as an Informed Craft   53

on the outcome of the experience and also on the nuances, sometimes implicit, of the lessons learned from student teaching. Beyond this, there are additional questions about the ownership of the classroom, the initiative to give over or retain control of the instruction, and the modeling that can be offered in this setting (does it support and encourage student teacher autonomy and learning?).

Cooperating teacher and student teacher relationships have the potential to enhance or inhibit the learning experience. However, in reality, it is not that straightforward given the presence of a third party in the learning process—the university supervisor. Under the assumption that most support and mentoring comes from the classroom teacher mentor, there was a time when the need for a university supervisor was questioned (Bowman, 1979; Rodgers & Keil, 2007; Wilson, 2006), yet university participation in the field experience portions of teacher preparation programs has continued. As a result, the triadic relationships between the university supervisor, cooperating teacher, and student teacher come together to create a unique energy that supports the field experience process. Supervisors must be able to build long-term relationships with the schools and classroom teachers they serve in order to be able to collaborate effectively to support student teachers (Jacobs et al., 2017; Slick, 1998a, 1998b).

Supervisors are in a novel position as the clear "third party" in the relationship—not present each day, not responsible for the education of the P–12 children in the classroom; the supervisor has the challenge of becoming part of the partnership from an outside position while honoring and supporting the needs of the student teacher (Slick, 1998b). Triads require a careful balance of perspectives and divergent needs to function successfully given the overlapping relationships that each person has with the others (Slick, 1998b). Supervisors ultimately play a crucial role for the triad in building the connections between the program intentions and the preservice teacher's experience in the field (Burns, Jacobs, & Yendol-Hoppey, 2016; Lee, 2011), supporting the cooperating teacher and student teacher in making sense of the expectations of the university's program, and encouraging program coherence (Jacobs et al., 2017; Slick, 1998b). Additionally, this can have a significant impact on the outcomes of the program in terms of achieving goals for quality teaching, and also on programmatic intentions such as commitments to equity and advocacy for change in the P–12 system. Supervisors support the communication between the various partners, share feedback with the cooperating teacher and the student teacher (Slick, 1998b), and assure that all program expectations are met both in quantity and quality of experiences (Koerner, Rust, & Baumgartner, 2002). Identifying ways to build this capacity in relationship building is crucial work for the supervisor, while maintaining the larger vision of the teacher candidate in the context of the program. This requires careful negotiation and renegotiation

54 Supervision as an Informed Craft

with the cooperating teacher throughout the period of the field experience (Slick, 1998b).

Johnston (2012) shares research on the experiences of Ben, a preservice student teacher, and Ms. T, a high school English teacher who served as Ben's cooperating teacher. With intention, Johnston placed Ben with a cooperating teacher who had differing views about effective instruction so Ben could learn the skills necessary for teacher agency through negotiation and renegotiation of best practice. This is not a traditional approach to candidate placement, intentionally supporting a misalignment in philosophy so a candidate can learn more about advocating for students through negotiation of teaching and learning with a cooperating teacher. Nevertheless, with careful support from the supervisor (Johnston), Ben was able to eventually reach an understanding with Ms. T about his ideas and how to engage them in the classroom in meaningful ways. While there may be valid questions about placing this level of responsibility on the candidate, if the rationale and supports are clear and present from the beginning, it might be possible to encourage agency on all parts. At the very least, their experience provides us with insight into the reflective learning that Johnston did as the supervisor, "I see now that I should teach candidates how to use initiative as a means to gain respect and trust *before* introducing ideas that may conflict with the status quo" (Johnston, 2012, p. 140). Recognizing this area for improvement can set the supervisor, the cooperating teacher, and the candidate up for a more effective experience in the future. Clear communication about these intentions allows for the development of agency with all partners in the clinical setting.

As a field, teacher education is embracing a range of clinically rich and intensive partnership models that require extensive and meaningful collaboration between schools and universities (AACTE, 2018; Jacobs et al., 2017; NCATE, 2010). Doing so has the potential to positively impact teacher education experiences for candidates, but also may change the parameters of the relationships required of supervisors and cooperating teachers, and other stakeholders in the placement. More is being asked of cooperating teachers in time spent with candidates, with others in their classrooms observing practice throughout the day, the nature or type of interaction that may be required with a university supervisor through accreditation mandates, and data or documentation requirements. Supervision should be carefully reenvisioned amidst these changes to further build productive relationships within the triad that build agency for all partners to be educational advocates for quality learning. Clear and thoughtful intentions around designing and implementing this work are required by all members of the triad (though particularly the cooperating teacher and the university supervisor). Purposeful and engaged conversation and clarity about mentoring practices are necessary on all fronts for a successful triadic relationship.

Influence of Content Areas

Innovation in best practice for teaching and learning is often determined by content area—what might work well in one academic area, and be cutting edge, might not work successfully in another disciplinary area. For supervisors, the nuances of content areas inform different types of feedback, guiding mentoring tailored to the needs of the discipline and the agency of the novice teacher (Bates & Burbank, 2008). Recent survey data about supervisor agency with instruction included a supervisor sharing her experiences in fostering innovation with the content:

> I think this is an important part of supervision. Getting students to realize it's not enough to simply teach the way it was taught to them is really critical. Part of my job is to get students to think about how to engage students in the content, and that requires innovation.
>
> (Bates & Burbank, 2018)

While supervisors see ways that they can play a role in supporting content innovation, it is often bounded by understanding that the cooperating teacher owns the classroom decisions in these areas that may limit the innovative or exploratory work done by student teachers (Bates & Burbank, 2018). Further, depending on state and university rules about appropriate supervisory assignments with regard to content areas (particularly in secondary education), supervisors who are supervising out of the content area where they have teaching expertise may feel less effective or at the very least less certain of what they may have to offer to the candidate (Burbank, Bates, & Gupta, 2016; Bullock, 2012; Slick, 1998a). This can have a negative impact on the perceptions and enactment of supervisor agency and is worth program-level reflection about the role of content expertise in supervisory practice. Research on content areas has identified certain benefits and drawbacks for a clear emphasis on content expertise in supervisory practice. How does the content area inform the nature of the supervision offered, and how does this work frame conversation and understanding around beliefs about knowledge?

Secondary education adds a layer of complexity to supervision because of a clear and careful need to address disciplinary knowledge issues. While these content distinctions are important in elementary education, and deserve the attention of the supervisor, the expertise of the supervisor is typically more focused on the pedagogy of elementary classroom students' needs. Elementary supervisors must demonstrate a knowledge base in a broad range of curricular and pedagogical areas rather than depth in one particular discipline-specific area like secondary supervisors. In secondary supervision experiences, guidance must be provided about teaching that intentionally and carefully intersects pedagogy with content knowledge (Shulman, 1986, 1987) to develop a range of knowledge

56 Supervision as an Informed Craft

bases in the novice educator. Teachers are held accountable for in-depth content knowledge to ensure adequate knowledge is provided to students (Ball, Thames, & Phelps, 2008; Hill, Rowne, & Ball, 2005; Ma, 1999) and to inform teacher accountability in education.

Research finds that student teachers value a balance between content expertise and general insight into pedagogy that informs classroom community and student diversity as well as management (Burbank et al., 2016; Burbank, Ramirez, & Bates, 2012). Findings show that "supervisory support that tethers pedagogy to content in explicit ways will likely provide conceptual anchors that allow for connections in preservice teachers' understanding of the relationship between curriculum and instruction" (Burbank et al., 2016, p. 63). As teacher candidates move through the teacher development growth process of "shifting" (Clandinin & Huber, 2005, p. 58) and evolving from novice to more seasoned expert, they are empowered through a balance in supervisory support for content and pedagogy.

Supervisors can demonstrate their agency in developing strategies that link content with pedagogy in ways that are individually meaningful to teacher candidates. Secondary teacher candidate participants in the research moved from a point of view that content was "the" thing that would make them successful in the classroom to becoming increasingly less confident over time about supporting students through pedagogical content knowledge (diversity needs, etc.) (Shulman, 1986, 1987), recognizing the need for insight and development that would foster more comprehensive and well-rounded classroom practices. This transitional process was particularly relevant for mathematics and science teacher candidates over those in the humanities. To support this growth over time, it is critical that supervisors must be able to and willing to provide evolving practices that meet each candidate at the spot of developmental readiness for that moment, knowing that it can and will shift. This may incorporate both content-specific models of supervisory support and generalist practices.

Utilizing professional agency to make mentoring decisions empowers supervisors to design conscious and intentional support strategies to model and reflect the work desired of teachers in responding to their students' needs. There are models of supervision that teacher education programs can use to ensure a range of topics are addressed through supervisory practices, building off candidate needs as well as program goals and expectations. There is no "one-size-fits-all stance for teaching and learning" (Burbank et al., 2016, p. 66) that can be adopted for supervisory practice. We must recognize the following in order to ensure that student teachers have quality experiences to support the learning:

> Without supervisory and mentoring support that is attuned to fine-grained understandings of teacher development with a specific focus

on content area influence, experience, and holistic views of teachers' work, supervisory support may be limited to generic teaching competencies and fail to demonstrate the complexity of professional knowledge.

(Burbank et al., 2016, p. 67)

Supervisors play a clear role in ensuring the tension between technical nuances and broader, more global issues of classroom diversity and student learning needs are constantly attended to in service of the long-range goals of teacher development. Supervisor agency must be used to support student teachers through these "shiftings" (Clandinin & Huber, 2005, p. 58), understanding that the uncertainty that may be experienced will help the novice educator make sense of the purpose of teaching and learning in schools today.

Research shows that content area expectations can influence attention to issues of classroom diversity (Burbank et al., 2012), often reinforcing assumptions about the norms of student demographics that are found in a given content area. For example, when the teacher candidate has no questions about the lack of racial or gender diversity of a chemistry class, as compared to the diversity of the school community, supervisors must use their agency to challenge the oversight and encourage the educator to acknowledge and problematize the situation in ways that may affect change over time in the community. Fostering critically reflective thinking can encourage the candidate to take a more complicated look at the situation and position the supervisor as an advocate for contemplation of these issues (Burbank et al., 2012). Identifying positions of agency for novice educators to merge the divide between pedagogy and content area can increase access to underrepresented communities in varied disciplines. Above all:

> The direction and guidance of supervisors and mentors must recognize the complexity of professional knowledge. Through this recognition, both teacher candidates and supervisors view the work of teachers through lenses that reveal the range of factors that influence teachers' work, thereby strengthening how issues in teaching are framed and examined.
>
> (Burbank et al., 2016, p. 67)

Culturally Responsive Supervision

Supervision requires complex understanding of the context in which the supervisory work is occurring (Bates et al., 2011; Levine, 2011). Recognizing and addressing elements of classroom diversity—varied languages spoken, the demographics of race, ethnicity, poverty status, etc.—is crucial to the support supervisors must provide to novice teachers. Attention

58 Supervision as an Informed Craft

to specific context requires nuanced responses to the candidate's learning needs while also supporting the unique needs of the teaching and learning environment. Ralph (2003) refers to this type of supervision as "contextual supervision" because of the focus on the context informing the actions that are taken through supervision. Models where supervisory relationships exist across multiple field experiences (Bullock, 2012) may be one way to foster the safe space necessary for exploration of complex topics like equity. Giving a supervisor and the teacher candidate enough time to get to know each other, build trusting relationships, and identify areas for growth, but also patterns of improvement, can result in the ongoing development of innovation and agency on the part of the candidate. "Feeling the power of one's voice is fundamentally connected with developing one's sense of agency" (Brookfield, 1995, p. 46), and this can be true for both supervisors and candidates. Agency is necessary during teacher preparation to shift the culture of schools toward responsive practices and find the reflective tools that help candidates build those skills that have been emphasized over the years (two seminal references for this work include: Brookfield, 1995; Zeichner & Liston, 1996).

Richardson (1996) determined that student teachers were more responsive to learning from challenging teaching dilemmas and producing alternatives for action when they confronted them in practice rather than during coursework. Yet, Hawkey (1997) learned that student teachers were often unsure about which perspective or advice to follow when confronted with varied opinions from cooperating teachers, university supervisors, etc. In her research, it was unclear how student teachers were making sense of the various opinions they were provided. Richardson's research shows that supervisors hired to support the teacher candidate throughout the field experience need to play a key role in helping student teachers unpack the dilemmas of teaching so that they generate the most possible options that encourage agency towards culturally responsive classroom practices.

Zeichner and Liston (1985) identified four approaches to the feedback offered by supervisors during post-observation debriefing conferences. Justificatory and critical discourse styles are two strategies that encourage the type of reflective thinking that fosters candidate growth around agency. Justificatory discourse focuses on asking candidates to identify why they have made certain decisions; in other words, addressing "why do this, in this way, with these particular students" (Zeichner & Liston, 1985, p. 163). Critical discourse moves the step further to address the underlying rationales used in the justification stage. It may also focus on the values in the curriculum and instruction—the hidden curriculum present in the classroom (Zeichner & Liston, 1985). This is all necessary work for teacher candidates to identify and address the equity issues that may be present in the nature of schooling. Supervisors must be able and willing to:

listen and support their [student teachers'] work, while challenging students to think, grow, and act as multicultural educators. As with children in schools, supervisors need to accept and get to know each student teacher and their cultural background, educational knowledge, and unique experiences.

(Grant & Zozakiewicz, 1995, pp. 271–272)

Addressing candidate readiness to teach students from diverse backgrounds requires supervisors to help candidates attend to their own status in society and reflect on how this can influence their teaching practices. If candidates are expected to act as agents of change, pushing schools and communities forward to respond to student diversity, they must first understand their own perspectives and experiences. According to Flessner et al. (2012), "An important form of agency is knowledge of self in order for individuals to (re)construct themselves within existing structures" (p. 173). Engaging work through teacher education can build this initial knowledge (e.g., through coursework activities such as oral histories [Blumenreich, 2012]) but it must also be actively applied in the field setting. At this point, the ideals and commitments of the teacher candidate often come into conflict with the cooperating teacher's perspective. As described earlier in the section on triadic relationships, the supervisor plays a strong negotiator role in helping the student teacher understand the needs of the cooperating teacher and vice versa. Through these ongoing negotiations, the supervisor can play a profound role in shaping the agency of the candidate, while valuing and encouraging the agency of the cooperating teacher as a model for creating communities of professional learners invested in teaching practice. This double layer of agency—on the part of the supervisor and eventually on the part of the candidate—is required to effect change.

Conclusion

University supervisors are in a unique and challenging position as they develop complex, nurtured relationships with cooperating teachers, school faculty, student teachers, and university program leadership. The supervisor must have a deep knowledge of self as a professional, recognizing the influences on supervisory practice brought forward from previous experiences, understanding how these experiences act on and impact current practices with novice educators, and showing both a commitment and a strategy to act as an agent of change for schools by working carefully and collaboratively with other educators. As Bullock (2012) states:

Part of a teacher educator's responsibility [. . .], is to find ways to help teacher candidates attend to problems of practice and their subsequent default reasons. Only by naming and interpreting default

60 *Supervision as an Informed Craft*

pedagogies can teacher candidates (or teacher educators) move toward enacting approaches that are significantly different from the approaches they experienced as students.

(p. 153)

Supervisors must acknowledge and work within the boundaries of content knowledge expertise while realizing creative strategies to flex those boundaries to provide broad, generalist knowledge about best practices for all students in order to ensure that classroom communities reflect the reality of modern society's diversity and inclusive nature. Reflective work, a thread throughout all aspects of this text, is crucial to actively engage in improving practice and identifying strategies that can foster ongoing development of both the supervisor and the novice educator.

References

American Association of Colleges of Teacher Education. (2018). *A pivot toward clinical practice, its lexicon, and the renewal of educator preparation.* Washington, DC: Author.

Anderson, D. (2007). The role of cooperating teachers' power in student teaching. *Education, 128*(2), 307–323.

Ball, D. L., Thames, M. H., & Phelps, G. (2008). Content knowledge for teaching: What makes it special? *Journal of Teacher Education, 59*(5), 389–407. doi:10.1177/0022487108324554

Bates, A. J., & Burbank, M. D. (2008). Effective student teacher supervision in the era of No Child Left Behind. *The Professional Educator, 32*(2), 1–11.

Bates, A. J., & Burbank, M. D. (2018, March). *Agency in teacher supervision and mentoring.* Paper presented at the annual conference of the American Association of Colleges of Teacher Education, Baltimore, MD.

Bates, A. J., Drits, D., & Ramirez, L. A. (2011). Self-awareness and enactment of supervisory stance: Influences on responsiveness toward student teacher learning. *Teacher Education Quarterly, 38*(3), 69–87.

Beck, C., & Kosnik, C. (2002). Components of a good practicum placement: Student teacher perceptions. *Teacher Education Quarterly, 29*(2), 91–98.

Blumenreich, M. (2012). Teacher learners' oral history projects: Exploring how our communities and cultural pasts shape us. In R. Flessner, G. R. Miller, K. M. Patrizio, & J. R. Horwitz (Eds.), *Agency through teacher education: Reflection, community, and learning.* New York, NY: Rowman & Littlefield Education.

Bowman, N. (1979). College supervisor of student teaching: A time to reconsider. *Journal of Teacher Education, 30*(3), 29–30.

Brookfield, S. (1995). *Becoming a critically reflective teacher.* San Francisco, CA: Jossey-Bass.

Bullock, S. M. (2012). Creating a space for the development of professional knowledge: A self- study of supervising teacher candidates during practicum placements. *Studying Teacher Education, 8*(2), 143–156. doi:10.1080/17425 964.2012.692985

Supervision as an Informed Craft 61

Burbank, M. D., Bates, A. J., & Gupta, U. (2016). The influence of teacher development on secondary content area supervision among preservice teachers. *The Teacher Educator, 51*(1), 55–69. doi:10.1080/08878730.2015.1107441

Burbank, M. D., Ramirez, L., & Bates, A. J. (2012). Critically reflective thinking in urban teacher education: A comparative case study of two participants' experiences as content specialists. *The Professional Educator, 36*(2), 24–41.

Burns, R. W., Jacobs, J., & Yendol-Hoppey, D. (2016). The changing nature of the role of the university supervisor and function of preservice teacher supervision in an era of clinically-rich practice. *Action in Teacher Education, 38*(4), 410–425.

Clandinin, D. J., & Huber, M. (2005). Shifting stories to live by: Interweaving the personal and professional in teachers' lives. In D. Beijjard, P. Meijer, G. Morine-Dershimer, & H. Tillma (Eds.), *Teacher professional development in changing conditions* (pp. 43–59). Dordrecht, The Netherlands: Springer.

Clift, R. T., & Brady, P. (2005). Research on methods courses and field experiences. In M. Cochran-Smith & K. Zeichner (Eds.), *Studying teacher education* (pp. 309–424). Mahwah, NJ: Lawrence Erlbaum Associates.

Flessner, R., Miller, G. R., Patrizio, K. M., & Horwitz, J. R. (2012). *Agency through teacher education: Reflection, community, and learning.* New York, NY: Rowman & Littlefield Education.

Friebus, R. J. (1977). Agents of socialization involved in student teaching. *Journal of Educational Research, 70,* 263–268.

Gimbert, B., & Nolan, J. F. (2003). The influence of the professional development school context on supervisory practice: A university supervisor's and interns' perspective. *Journal of Curriculum and Supervision, 18*(4), 353–379.

Glenn, W. (2006). Model versus mentor: Defining the necessary qualities of the effective cooperating teacher. *Teacher Education Quarterly, 33*(1), 85–95.

Grant, C. A., & Zozakiewicz, C. A. (1995). Student teachers, cooperating teachers, and supervisors: Interrupting the multicultural silences of student teaching. In J. M. Larkin & C. E. Sleeter (Eds.), *Developing multicultural teacher education curricula* (pp. 259–278). Albany, NY: State University of New York Press.

Hawkey, K. (1997). Roles, responsibilities, and relationships in mentoring: A literature review and agenda for research. *Journal of Teacher Education, 48*(5), 325–335.

Hill, H. C., Rowne, B., & Ball, D. L. (2005). Effects of teachers' mathematical knowledge for teaching on student achievement. *American Educational Research Journal, 42*(2), 371–406. doi:10.3102/0002 8312042002371

Jacobs, J., Hogarty, K., & Burns, R. W. (2017). Elementary preservice teacher field supervision: A survey of teacher education programs. *Action in Teacher Education, 39*(2), 172–186. doi:10.1080/01626620.2016.1248300

Johnston, J. (2012). "I want to test my own unique ideas": Tensions in the candidate-cooperating teacher relationship. In R. Flessner, G. R. Miller, K. M. Patrizio, & J. R. Horwitz (Eds.), *Agency through teacher education: Reflection, community, and learning.* New York, NY: Rowman & Littlefield Education.

Koerner, M., Rust, F. O., & Baumgartner, F. (2002). Exploring roles in student teaching placements. *Teacher Education Quarterly, 29*(2), 35–58.

Lee, Y. A. (2011). Self-study of cross-cultural supervision of teacher candidates for social justice. *Studying Teacher Education, 7*(1), 3–18. doi:10.1080/1742 5964.2011.558341

62 Supervision as an Informed Craft

Levine, T. H. (2011). Features and strategies of supervisor professional community as a means of improving the supervision of preservice teachers. *Teaching and Teacher Education, 27*(5), 930–941.

Lindgren, U. (2005). Experiences of beginning teachers in a school-based mentoring program in Sweden. *Educational Studies, 31*(3), 251–263. http://dx.doi.org/10.1080/03055690500236290

Ma, L. (1999). *Knowing and teaching elementary mathematics.* Mahwah, NJ: Lawrence Erlbaum Associates.

Marable, M. A., & Raimondi, S. L. (2007). Teachers' perceptions of what was most (and least) supportive during their first year of teaching. *Mentoring and Tutoring: Partnership in Learning, 15*(1), 25–37. http://dx.doi.org/10.1080/13611260601037355

Miller, G. R., & McIntyre, C. (2012). Agency as critical reflection. In R. Flessner, G. R. Miller, K. M. Patrizio, & J. R. Horwitz (Eds.), *Agency through teacher education: Reflection, community, and learning.* New York, NY: Rowman & Littlefield Education.

National Council for Accreditation of Teacher Education. (2010). *Transforming teacher education through clinical practice: A national strategy to prepare effective teachers.* Washington, DC: Blue Ribbon Panel on Clinical Preparation and Partnerships for Improved Student Learning.

Newell, G. E., & Connors, S. P. (2011). "Why do you think that?" A supervisor's mediation of a preservice English teacher's understanding of instructional scaffolding. *English Education, 43*(3), 225–261.

Ralph, E. G. (2003). Enhancing mentorship in the practicum: Improving contextual supervision. *McGill Journal of Education, 38*(1), 28–48.

Richardson, V. (1996). The role of attitudes and beliefs in learning to teach. In J. Sikula (Ed.), *Handbook of research on teacher education* (pp. 102–119). New York, NY: Palgrave Macmillan.

Rodgers, A., & Keil, V. L. (2007). Restructuring a traditional student teacher supervision model: Fostering enhanced professional development and mentoring within a professional development school context. *Teaching and Teacher Education, 23*(1), 63–80. doi:10.1016/j.tate.2006.04.012

Rozelle, J. J., & Wilson, S. M. (2012). Opening the black box of field experiences: How cooperating teachers' beliefs and practices shape student teachers' beliefs and practices. *Teaching and Teacher Education, 28*(8), 1196–1205. http://dx.doi.org/10.1016.j.tate.2012.07.008

Rust, F. O. (1988, March–April). How supervisors think about teaching. *Journal of Teacher Education, 56*–64.

Shulman, L. (1986). Those who understand: Knowledge growth in teaching. *Educational Researcher, 15*(2), 4–14.

Shulman, L. (1987). Knowledge and teaching: Foundations of the new reform. *Harvard Educational Review, 57,* 1–22. doi:10.3102/0013189X015002004

Slick, S. K. (1998a). The university supervisor: A disenfranchised outsider. *Teaching and Teacher Education, 14*(8), 821–834.

Slick, S. K. (1998b). A university supervisor negotiates territory and status. *Journal of Teacher Education, 49*(4), 306–315.

Stanulis, R. N., & Floden, R. E. (2009). Intensive mentoring as a way to help beginning teachers develop balanced instruction. *Journal of Teacher Education, 60*(2), 112–122. http://dx.doi.org/10/1177/0022487108330553

Veal, M. L., & Rikard, L. (1998). Cooperating teachers' perspective on the student teaching triad. *Journal of Teacher Education, 49*(2), 108–119.

Weiss, E. M., & Weiss, S. (2001). Doing reflective supervision with student teachers in a professional development school culture. *Reflective Practice, 2,* 125–154. doi:10.1080/14623940120071343

Williams, J., Ritter, J., & Bullock, S. M. (2012). Understanding the complexity of becoming a teacher educator: Experience, belonging, and practice within a professional learning community. *Studying Teacher Education, 8*(3), 245–260. doi:10.1080/17425964.2012.719130

Wilson, E. K. (2006). The impact of an alternative model of student teacher supervision: Views of the participants. *Teaching & Teacher Education, 22*(1), 22–31. doi:10.1016/j.tate.2005.07.007

Zahorik, J. A. (1988). The observing-conferencing role of university supervisors. *Journal of Teacher Education, 39*(2), 9–16.

Zeichner, K. M., & Liston, D. P. (1985). Varieties of discourse in supervisory conferences. *Teaching and Teacher Education, 1*(2), 155–174.

Zeichner, K. M., & Liston, D. P. (1996). *Reflective teaching: An introduction.* Mahwah, NJ: Lawrence Erlbaum Associates.

Zeichner, K. M., & Tabachnick, B. R. (1982). The belief systems of university supervisors in an elementary student teaching program. *Journal of Education for Teaching, 8,* 34–54.

Zimpher, N. L., DeVoss, G., & Nott, D. (1980). A closer look at university student teacher supervision. *Journal of Teacher Education, 31*(4), 11–15.

4 Technology Integration in Supervision

In today's classrooms and schools, the daily work for educators is multifaceted and complex. Curriculum transfer, support of learners from diverse communities, and methodologies that include the integration of varied forms of technology are among the dimensions that contribute to the fabric of teaching. This chapter examines the different ways supervisors engage with technology integration as a vehicle for enhancing efficiency in communication and, more important, in developing agency. Through the implementation of technology, supervisors serve as conduits who engender cohesion, reflection, and coordination among communities of educators. In these ways, technology provides a mechanism for advancing professional agency among individuals and groups.

Goals of Technology Integration and Teacher Supervision

Technology integration as part of supervision offers a tool to enhance both teaching and professional decision-making. In line with the objectives of this text, technology within the context of supervision contributes to communication among communities of educators. The tools for enhancing dialogue allow mentors to create novel and in-depth experiences for teachers that encourage individual agency through their reflections on and reviews of teaching practices.

In their roles, mentors are uniquely poised to share insights on teaching and to encourage perspective-taking within public forums. Central to their work is guiding the scope and depth of feedback, facilitating opportunities for information sharing, and supporting analyses of teaching. Technology's role in advancing these particular goals takes place through enhanced dialogue, alterative formats for discussions and collaboration, and experiences that promote skill development in ways that are active and dynamic.

More Than Bells and Whistles

Historically, technology integration within educational spheres served to transmit data through relatively cost-effective means (Florell, 2016;

Rousmaniere, 2014). Early technology integration included methods for increasing professional communication through email, later with texting or instant messaging platforms, and more recently through video and web-based conferencing. While these tools are certainly contemporary, how they are used is key to enhancing educators' work and their agency as informed professionals.

For supervisors who infuse technology when working with preservice and in-service teachers, there is an inherent balancing act that requires attention to both teacher skill development as well as opportunities where technology supports in-depth reflection on teachers' work. To reach these goals requires both an acknowledgment of the technique-based uses of technology as well as technology used as a means of promoting inquiry and exploration. When technology infusion offers more than skill development, reflection and critical thinking must be nurtured and fostered. In order to enhance a more in-depth approach to teacher support, supervisors and mentors are essential in guiding the process of technology integration in their work with teachers. To reach this goal, technology, as a form of professional development, must be seen as more than skill acquisition.

Over time, technological advances have provided mentors with a myriad of ways to strengthen the types, frequency, and scope of feedback. For example, e-conversations among educators from across communities allow for collaborative explorations in areas such as curriculum and instruction within media-rich learning environments (e.g., smartboards, iPads, smartphones; e-readers) (Callahan, Saye, & Brush, 2015; Llinares, & Valls, 2007).

Unlike face-to-face conversations, which are typically based upon immediate recollections of lesson happenings, videos or virtual feedback may serve as a valuable tool for mentors that expand scope and audience. Captured lessons invite examinations of teaching through vignettes followed by commentary, reflection, and interactions between individual teachers, their observers, and a wider audience of educators.

Electronic formats also allow for more frequent periodic and informal reviews of teaching episodes. Advances from earlier times expanded participation. Past tools such as bug-in-the-ear devices provided mentors the opportunity to move from relatively didactic formats to interactive tools, including in situ reviews between a teacher and a supervisor or mentor (Gallant & Thyer, 2008). While important, the advice provided was typically procedural and rarely addressed reflection and attention to the range of variables that impact professional decision-making.

Expansions in the type of electronic venues in which supervisors and mentors engage also opened the audience of reviewers, particularly when group feedback was sought. A more fine-grained analysis revealed that the convenience of electronic formats allowed for professional conversations as mentors and teachers considered nuanced analyses of teaching

66 Technology Integration in Supervision

quality with specific indicators in mind (e.g., lesson delivery, assessment, learner differences, and classroom dynamics). For supervisors, the process of looking beyond technical skills increased agency as mentors advanced in their ability to guide and lead other professionals as experts and informed decision makers (Herrington, Herrington, Mantei, Olney, & Ferry, 2009).

Supervisory Support Beyond Technique Development

Regardless of the tool used, training and comfort levels must be considered when infusing electronic formats into supervisory and mentoring practices (Benko, Guise, Earl, & Gill, 2016; Curran, 2014). Even when individuals are familiar with tools such as email, blogs, and Twitter, research suggests electronic enhancements require systematic plans to address user practices (Brown, Higgins, & Hartley, 2001; Florell, 2016). Because of what is best described as anxiety for some teachers as they consider technology integration, many users inflate the time it takes/will take to engage in various e-formats. They specifically cite feelings of "fear" when trying to implement tools (Brown et al., 2001; Florell, 2016). As such, dedicated training and scaffolding provide both basic instruction for use and guidance to outline the purpose and value of various electronic formats. These levels of support thereby encourage opportunities for greater depth and scope of reflective practices (Brown et al., 2001; Florell, 2016).

Opportunities and Challenges

For educators to use technology to capture teaching episodes presents a unique set of opportunities and challenges. A positive opportunity is the access to teaching demonstrations across settings and over time that provides vantage points for pinpointing teaching practices in ways that are in-depth and specific. A challenge with reviews using technology is to ensure that teaching episodes allow for comprehensive discussions of quality based on collaboratively developed expectations. For example, a strength of contemporary video systems are features that allow educators to isolate teaching snapshots using video and audio annotations. These tools invite individuals or groups for feedback (Maheu, Pulier, McMenamin, & Posen, 2012). Clearly, these advances provide inclusive access to teaching at the micro level (e.g., still shots of interactions) and allow for storage and in-text annotations of teaching (e.g., Edthena). These particular features have the potential to contribute to rich and complex analyses of teaching. Further, the opportunity to annotate and isolate areas for feedback provides agency for the mentor or the teacher to develop purposeful goals around their own improvement and learning

Experiences where teachers revisit teaching provide mentors with opportunities to guide thinking in ways that promote conceptual examinations of teaching (i.e., building reflective practice), as well as offering recommendations on how to enhance technical skills and insights gained from feedback by peers (e.g., teacher blogs, sharing lesson plans). These review practices are particularly useful for beginners as they often require immediate suggestions for problem solving and expediency in communication (i.e., evenings when time is more flexible vs. during the teaching day) (Gareis & Nussbaum-Beach, 2007).

The question remains as to whether components of technological advances in supervision and mentoring add value that promotes in-depth reflections on practice. In order to develop the breadth and depth of how teaching is analyzed, supervisors must facilitate thought through questions, recommendations, and interpretations of the meaning behind these episodes. In these situations, technology is used to encourage deep reflection and facilitate discussions and reflections as part of a larger community. However, this process is dependent upon careful planning and attention to detail. Virtual mentoring has clear advantages when educators are in the position to think deeply and consider the range of factors that influence educators' work. These levels of reflection provide more than simple recaps of teaching episodes, but how does this happen?

In a study comparing virtual mentoring and face-to-face experiences, Bagley and Shaffer (2015) discuss the benefits of online mentoring when specific conditions are put into place. Specifically, when teachers are asked to observe video episodes of typical classroom teaching, researchers noted an advantage of the video format in observers' comments; that is, feedback from teacher observers was more candid. Because the teaching episodes did not involve people they knew, participating teachers and supervisors were able to consider the complexity of classroom problem-solving and decision-making processes more objectively. Further, the more objective episode reviews prompted conversation and problem-solving in ways that relied on knowledge of best practice without the fear of critiques based upon participant's own teaching. In these settings, the expertise and candid appraisals gave teachers increased levels of authority over recommendations without concern or emotion. This ownership of expertise in decision-making underscores the potential for building agency in professional decision-making with others. The value of mentoring and supervision within the context of teacher groups cannot be overestimated.

Power of Virtual Communities of Practice

Teacher supervisors are typically identified because they have experience teaching (Jacobs, Hogarty, & Burns, 2017). Supervisors being "on call" provides novices not only ready-and-willing colleagues, but professionals

68 *Technology Integration in Supervision*

who are able to provide resources and prompts for reflection on decision-making. Through the support provided by mentors, teachers are guided in their perspective-taking, thus encouraging agency as an element affecting change.

Discussions and reviews of teaching are often person or situation specific because the contexts of educators' work are complex and influenced by a range of variables. As such, face-to-face mentoring may be limited in that mentoring relationships are likely to be heavily informed by the personalities and the dynamics of people and individual settings. While certainly useful for problem solving and discussion, reflection in these situations may be confined to the parameters of individual contexts and the perspectives of the supervisor and mentee.

In order to broaden teachers' thinking, electronic communities provide a mechanism to examine teaching from multiple perspectives. This process of perspective taking moves reflections from typical problem-solving activities that may be fixed or narrow in focus. While immediate problem-solving is important (e.g., effective questioning strategies), teacher agency is enhanced when educators engage in perspective-taking that invites teachers to navigate complex environments and issues (e.g., trends in student performance based upon gender or race). Widening viewpoints provided by technology encourages educators to develop voice and to consider perspectives in ways that differ from face-to-face interactions where decision-making is typically focused on immediate dilemmas (Berry, 2007).

While face-to-face mentoring and support have been dubbed the "gold standard" for feedback on teaching (Florell, 2016), it does not have to stand in juxtaposition with virtual formats; that is, virtual supervisory and mentoring support are not an either or option for mentors and supervisors. Research on the efficacy of e-mentoring, while often a method of convenience, also exposes both strengths and inherent limitations if the systems are simply used as electronic transfers of feedback in ways that are similar to face-to-face communication (Jaffe, Moir, Swanson, & Wheeler, 2006). For example, virtual systems used in isolation may be limited if they are only used as an entrée into spaces where educators think and act in relatively predictable ways via question-posing and problem-solving among colleagues near and far. To extend these more predictable use of virtual dialogues for both preservice and in-service teachers, supervisors must encourage dedicated conversations, assessments, and dialogue on topics that are less perfunctory (Gareis & Nussbaum-Beach, 2007). These actions by mentors are particularly valuable in promoting teacher agency by sharing insights and perspectives quickly and collaboratively. Immediate reviews of teaching and the subsequent cataloging of feedback formalizes the process of capturing and reacting to teaching in new ways (e.g., record keeping, dialogue analyses).

Beyond practical advantages of expediency and storage, contemporary dialogue spaces have the potential to extend thinking beyond problem-solving through conversations within communities of practice (Lave & Wenger, 1990). Within these environments, situated learning reflects contexts, cultures, and the specific activities in which individuals engage. For teachers in these settings, a social process is informed by individuals in customized contexts within electronic communities. These outcomes are particularly important because they help combat isolation as a long-standing challenge within the profession (Jackson, 1990; Lortie, 2002).

As with most components of education, outcomes do not occur in isolation. In order to build supervisory support that encourages growth beyond more superficial problem-solving, supervisory relationships must be planned, communal, and monitored. Further, while technology integration encourages a range of information sharing experiences, reflection must remain central to discussions and individual decision-making (Florell, 2016).

Technology infusion among groups of educators is a way to increase dialogue between supervisors and novice teachers. Opportunities for greater reflection may be strengthened when mentors facilitate reflection and thoughtful consideration of teaching (Berry & Nussbaum-Beach, 2006). Expanding dialogue to include a range of viewpoints increases exchanges as opportunities for perspective-taking (Alliance for Excellent Education, 2004; Kapadia, Coca, & Easton, 2007; Wegner, McDermott, & Snyder, 2002).

The spirit of being part of a shared commitment to the education of P–12 students fosters opportunities that are typically absent when collaboration and conversation are limited to individuals or a small cohort of colleagues and mentors. For example, online collaborations have a long-standing history of building leadership potential, encouraging perspective sharing, and enlisting peer support (Hawkes & Rosmiszowski, 2001; Jervis, 1996). Through the shared story of teachers' work, e-communities place educators and their supervisors in the unique position of unearthing teaching through closer reviews and reflection as members of professional systems (i.e., with their supervisors, local peers, and distant colleagues).

Reflection and Decision-Making Through Virtual Supervision and Mentoring

While there are obvious advantages of efficiency from electronic guidance, supervisors must also take care in how communication is orchestrated. Mentors must attend to how they will build virtual experiences with teachers in ways that account for the interpersonal dimensions that are sometimes lost in electronic environments (Rousmaniere, 2014).

70 Technology Integration in Supervision

Florell (2016) suggests face-to-face meetings as the first step in building relationships and moving toward more long-term relationships that will include face-to-face, hybrid, and possibly fully asynchronous support. As with any relationship, creating a foundation that includes dialogue, ground rules for participation, and an explanation of how tools will be used are essential dimensions of productive experiences.

A 2007 study by Gareis and Nussbaum-Beach further highlights the critical need for mentor-led facilitation that is designed to build community between participants. Within the context of their study, preservice teachers were provided with key elements of support via an online format that includes what the authors identified as: (1) vocational support for transitions into a career; (2) psychosocial support; and (3) role modeling. Together, these components allowed for group support that extended beyond what is typically provided beginning teachers. Further, the mentor's attention to communication strategies enhanced virtual discussions that were initially focused topics and exchanges that prompted, challenged, and referenced resources and research on topics of interest. Over time, as beginning teachers developed the skills to situate their specific needs with colleagues, these scaffolds were lessened in ways that encouraged ownership. The advantages of an electronic paper trail were particularly useful in documenting growth over time.

Study data from participants also highlighted how the content of electronic postings changed over time for beginning teachers (Gareis & Nussbaum-Beach, 2007). Within the context of this online environment, mentors were part of a community of learners versus the more traditional role of directing or advising a novice teacher. This finding is significant as it speaks to supervision as a vehicle for promoting ownership and agency among educators who work together. The authors' description of virtual community networks reflects the power of educators coming together for decision-making across curriculum, instruction, and assessment.

Electronic Supervision for Skill and Community Building

As many educators are aware, group dynamics do not happen on their own. Within supervisory relationships, deliberate requests for group involvement must be facilitated by supervisors. Central to their goal is fostering community interdependence that acknowledges educators as knowledgeable and capable of contributing to others' success. Supervisors offer unique contributions to push greater depth in discussions, and create supported opportunities for risk-taking and decision-making. These dimensions allow for greater empowerment by those engaged in these experiences. An example of specific actions are seen when teachers use electronic readers as a vehicle for enhancing their content knowledge and a tool for shared analyses (Charbonneau-Gowdy, Capredoni, Gonzalez, Jayo, & Raby, 2016).

In their study Charbonneau-Gowdy et al. (2016) identified the benefits of electronic communities where beginning teachers and their mentors engaged in electronic contexts for information sharing and reflection. As mentioned, technology integration as part of mentoring and supervision requires a balance between providing teachers with tools of practice and a format designed to build cadres of educators committed to common goals. For the teachers in the Charbonneau-Gowdy (2016) study, community networks were created using electronic e-readers covering topics that addressed the language development of teachers enhancing their knowledge (i.e., using technology as a tool of practice) as well as a vehicle for community building. The Online Community Network system met two goals: (1) to enhance the English language skills of teachers through the use of e-readers within a community working on the same goal and (2) to provide an electronic forum where supervisors mentored teachers to explore various texts on language acquisition using online discussions. The benefits of the e-readers and online discussions included accessing specific texts designed to improve literacy skills and participation with peers across communities who were also developing similar skills (i.e., beginning teachers, English literacy).

E-readers also provided subsequent mentoring through the creation of professional networks for idea sharing, a venue for exploring suggestions for practice, and the establishment of a community for educators to experience scenarios similar to those within their own teaching. Cohorts offer a venue for publically shared ownership and agency in professional decision-making. To this end, electronic supervisory support was particularly valuable in facilitating access to additional curriculum on language skill acquisition and guidance designed to increase confidence, competencies, and agency among preservice teachers (Charbonneau-Gowdy et al., 2016). For the mentors, their communication skills were essential to the success of these professional mentoring relationships.

Dedicated Skills for Technology Integration

To be effective, supervisors and mentors must possess a strong knowledge base, as well as the skills necessary for effective communication. Research by Leibold and Schwarz (2015) highlights the importance of feedback within the contexts of online environments. For example, generic feedback on skill development often includes corrective feedback; epistemic feedback (prompts); suggestive feedback; and epistemic, suggestive feedback (prompts with recommendations) (Alvarez, Espasa, & Guasch, 2011). The goals of these message types vary, but are generally designed to facilitate greater reflection over time, moving from technical skill development to more in-depth thinking about teaching (Callahan et al., 2015). When guidance is provided through prompting, challenging, and encouraging greater depth in discussions, the benefits for teachers include

72 *Technology Integration in Supervision*

greater self-efficacy and overall receptivity. The use of rubrics and templates strengthens feedback through structures and parameters for sharing information with specific goals identified for reflection and further consideration (Bonnel & Boehm, 2011; Jamison, 2004).

In addition to feedback types, practical courtesies and habits of practice underscore the importance of communication etiquette. Specifically, regardless of the electronic format (e.g., Twitter, email, blogs) those in professional settings should be provided with explicit guidelines for communication and expectations for participation and information sharing. While most feedback is in written form, audio feedback personalizes and motivates teachers (i.e., tone of voice; emphasis and nuanced dimensions of each individual) (Todd, 2012). As a rule, feedback that is positive in tone, timely, and specific is typically well received. These recommendations are particularly critical when keeping the goal of community central to interactions between educators. Finally, supervisory agency is a process that may be deepened by capturing the intent and emotion that are part of teaching. Incorporating the sometimes subtle dimensions of mentoring and supervision contributes to meaningful support. The human side of teachers' work reflects individuality and reactions to the characteristics of teaching environments. These emphases are particularly critical in environments requiring explicit data for individual teachers and for those working in unique and specialized settings.

Special Education

The contexts of classrooms and the individuality of students with disabilities require a specialized skill set among mentors. For example, within special education settings, teachers are responsible for extensive documentation and collaboration related to planning, policy compliance, and communication with colleagues and caregivers. Specific mentoring and supervisory tasks include sharing information when specialized curricula support and teaching methods are required in areas including, but not limited to, computer assistive technology, text enhancers, and various learning programs (Israel, Knowlton, Griswold, & Rowland, 2009; Smith & Israel, 2010). For mentors, e-formats offer platforms where access to information and resources for communities of teachers can be specifically dedicated to support and address the needs of children with disabilities that align with the expectations delineated within students' Individualized Education Plans (IEPs). Because families and other service providers are integral to student support, mentors are positioned to bring together the compliment of stakeholders who contribute to students' education goals.

Diverse Educator Communities

The value of electronic communities is evident in their potential to bring together educators. These outcomes are particularly important for individuals who are either physically distanced from others (e.g., rural communities), distanced in access to peers within a content area (e.g., science), or members of underrepresented communities (e.g., teachers of color) (Berry, 2007). The advantages of electronic spaces offer these teachers and mentors linkages when local colleagues are sometimes few in number or nonexistent. These needs are particularly noticeable for people of color and women in content areas such as science, mathematics, and engineering (Bierema & Hill, 2005).

Professional camaraderie among colleagues-at-a distance may be facilitated through peer and supervisory dialogue where educators experience an accessible space to collaborate and network beyond personal contacts (Berry, 2007). Within these contexts, supervisors facilitate conversations and share resources among communities with specialized interests, backgrounds, and identities. Mentors are in the unique position of facilitating opportunities that connect educators through resources, collegial community building, and prompts that address the challenges of working in sometimes isolated cadres. For many, simply having the support of other educators motivates and underscores membership in a wider community and increases agency as result of being part of a larger effort.

Social Media

A contemporary iteration of past platforms for communication is evidenced in the use of Twitter. Personal Learning Networks (PLN) emerged in the early 2000s as a format that allows users to self-create learning opportunities using reflection to meet the daily needs of individuals (Downes, 2009). As a current means of connecting, the format is particularly relevant for beginning teachers who are likely familiar with the technology (Benko et al., 2016). While data collection on the utility of Twitter is somewhat limited, its novelty is relevant to varied audiences. Its pedagogical utility focuses attention to in-action teaching between individual communities and those at a distance in ways other methods of communication are not able to capture (Curran, 2014).

A year-long study of a novice teachers' use of Twitter identified nuances as a mentoring tool (Risser, 2013). The study examined the frequency of use, cohort of users, and changes in the teacher's network of users over time (Risser, 2013). Findings reflect considerations when implementing Twitter as a tool with specific attention to sharing resources among educators, versus a platform for questions and answers.

Benko and colleagues (2016) suggest that Twitter, similar to more traditional reflection practices (e.g., journaling), allows supervisors to guide questions and responses that are quite focused, thereby reducing meandering within discussions through quick prompts. To encourage greater depth, follow-up on the questions and prompts allows for more in-depth reviews. The chat option, for example, creates an environment with peers that has the potential to decrease anxiety and pressure at times when

74 *Technology Integration in Supervision*

novice teachers find themselves feeling overwhelmed (Benko et al., 2016). However, without guided practice that aligns with larger goals for reflection, teachers may struggle with Twitter and rely on it as only a quick-fix problem-solving devoid of depth, reflection, and critical analysis (Doyle, 2015).

As with any form of technology integration, implementing Twitter as a mentoring or supervisory tool requires a systematic process where instruction and scaffolding are necessary. When supervisors provide teachers with guidance on how to connect with colleagues, Twitter forces succinct and focused dialogue. The limited character availability in Twitter requires brevity and focus in-the-moment.

As a means of advancing informal learning within electronic communities of peers, one researcher reports that Twitter creates opportunities for individuals to be part of larger public networks in ways that support learning (Gilbert, 2016). The study's attention to the relationships and community building between network members highlights the tool's use as fluid and a means of enhancing efficacy—a factor for mentors to consider when establishing professional learning communities.

Practical Considerations

The public nature of social media creates opportunities that enhance communication between teachers and their mentors (Berry, 2007). However, as with all forms of public communication, caution is warranted regarding privacy and confidentiality in information sharing. The Family Educational Rights and Privacy Act (FERPA) often serves as the gatekeeper for the types of information that may be shared and for what purpose within the contexts of P–12 settings, particularly student data. Additionally, because electronic supervision and mentoring may incorporate student images, users must ensure proper permissions are acquired in compliance with various stakeholder policies for access and distribution.

The range of technology options when supervising and evaluating teachers' work reflects the multifaceted components of contemporary systems. For example, videos, in-text note taking and annotation, as well as data storage within these systems are more commonplace than in the past. These levels of complexity challenge both those using these tools and the teachers on the receiving end. As such, both groups are responsible for determining how "data" are gathered, for what purposes, and how information is parsed and evaluated (Maheu et al., 2012).

Confidentiality must also be considered when determining formats for information storage. While relatively static episodes of teaching through photos or video snapshots were common in the past, these artifacts have given way to more complex layers of performance as well as the types of feedback shared by supervisors and evaluators (Florell, 2016). Because technology affords multiple ways to represent teaching, educators must be vigilant in how they address the custodial responsibilities for information sharing. Minimally, though critically important, users must understand how data remain secure.

In preparation for supervisory support using virtual storage, supervisors and their mentees must be aware of policies, liabilities, and the potential for information to be shared within public venues, whether or not these outcomes are intended (Florell, 2016). Cloud storage is one example of the changing face of data collection, particularly for video storage. However, even under the best of circumstances, as with many technologies, cloud systems are limited in their levels of security (Rousmaniere, 2014).

A Worldwide Audience

Those working with student teachers and in-service teachers must recognize the inherent reality of how information is managed, and that no electronic format is 100% secure. Facebook, among other platforms, prompts a unique set of considerations for users within education communities. Aragon and Kaminski's 2012 study on ethical considerations using Facebook for communication revealed preservice teachers' impressions of Facebook posts and the implications of content regarding professional and ethical behaviors. Study findings highlight the platform's potential to encourage anonymity or autonomy among users in their expressions of beliefs and viewpoints (Aragon & Kaminski, 2012). A significant limitation of anonymous settings was the increased presence of statements identified as unethical and racist in nature (Aragon & Kaminski, 2012).

Research on communication within online settings highlights anonymity as a feature of users' thinking when taking part in feedback sharing. Within these settings users may engage in an unbridled sense of freedom in their commentary (Christopherson, 2007). These conclusions link to the work of others who cite data on prejudiced behaviors that are manifest when individuals believe that their viewpoints will not be linked to them personally (Coffey & Woolworth, 2004; Scheuruch & Young, 1997). The assumption that electronic communication guarantees anonymity is unlikely. The potential for information sharing in relatively anonymous environments may be particularly damaging if ground rules are not established in advance and maintained over time (Aragon & Kaminski, 2012; Cornelius, Gordon, & Harris, 2011). An assumed "freedom" within virtual communities must be considered carefully as more typical filters regarding the intention, audience, or impact may be overlooked (Leibold & Schwarz, 2015).

Data that illustrate users' perceptions of autonomy when using public media deserve the attention of mentors for multiple reasons. Foremost, education communities must consider the troubling reality of

76 *Technology Integration in Supervision*

belief systems that are racist or discriminatory. While it is important that these belief systems are challenged with explicit attention to how these values impact students and others in P–12, it is essential that educators understand their membership in a public profession. As such, stakeholder viewpoints are vast and varied. More practically, educators must understand the ever present public nature of their work and that electronic information sharing is always public.

When educators hold beliefs that are biased against individuals or groups, it is incumbent upon mentors to confront these behaviors. The manner in which these discussions take place may include a range of formats including course curricula, advisory roles, or as part of evaluation (Burbank, Ramirez, & Bates, 2016). Teachers who understand the range of factors that influence their work are better equipped to teach in ways that are informed and comprehensive. Dialogue within educational communities serves as one way of posing questions, and challenging thinking from multiple perspectives and viewpoints. Mentors who facilitate reflective thinking within complex scenarios are invaluable to advancing individual teaching specifically, and the profession, in general.

While there are clear limitations to environments where perceptions of anonymity absolve users of their responsibilities for actions and beliefs, anonymous environments also provide opportunities. A 2011 study by Cornelius and colleagues notes the benefits of electronic formats in allowing educators to tackle issues in ways that encourage freedom to experiment with decision-making and position-taking through role-play. Here, teachers are afforded perspective-taking experiences, and candor in sharing feedback that would otherwise be intimidating in face-to-face interactions. Additionally, role-play or scenario reviews allow supervisors to deconstruct teaching challenges that may reflect those of their mentees (Cornelius et al., 2011).

Technology and Performance Assessment: Opportunities and Challenges

Defining quality remains a priority for those in education communities as part of contemporary policy and decision-making. While the concept of quality is certainly a long-standing value within the profession, as discussed in Chapter 1 of this text, how quality is identified and documented has evolved over the past 30 years. At present, performance-based assessments outline specific methods to determine teacher quality through identified criteria incorporated in portfolios, data gained through observations, and videos of teaching (Coggshall, Max, & Bassett, 2008; Darling-Hammond & Snyder, 2000; Florell, 2016).

Advocates of performance-based assessment highlight the utility of evaluation measures that are authentic and presented over time (Darling-Hammond & Snyder, 2000). Efforts to assemble teaching competencies, theoretically, allow for holistic and comprehensive demonstrations of teaching quality using technological tools that allow for reviews and evaluations of teaching in ways that are valid and reliable (Wei & Pechone, 2010).

Beginning in the early 2000s federal and state mandates on teacher quality moved the needle on the types of performance assessment required of educators. For example, recommendations by the U.S. Department of Education (DOE) for evaluating teacher quality call for explicit indicators linked to standardized performance assessment (DOE, 2016). Further, national and state accreditation mandates challenge teacher preparation programs and districts to strategically document teachers' work in many ways (Council for the Accreditation of Educator Preparation, 2017).

Within the past 10 years, formal documentation of teachers' work includes state-based standardized assessment tools, as well as electronic portfolios (Castle & Shaklee, 2006; Wise, Ehrenberg, & Leibbrand, 2008; Coggshall et al., 2008). These evaluation systems are specifically designed to capture and review teaching using explicit frameworks and a range of evaluation criteria. Increasingly, video episodes are included within portfolio systems because they provide opportunities for teachers to reflect on their practice through reviews of teaching. They also provide a medium to determine quality and invite discussion as part of more comprehensive performance assessments.

Performance assessments are central to teacher evaluations where data may take a number of formats including in-person or video reviews of teaching that capture specific areas identified for review and assessment. At their core, performance assessments are designed to identify the impact of daily teaching on student learning. For supervisors, a component of their role may include evaluating teacher quality within the context of these assessment efforts (Wei & Pechone, 2010). Electronic rubrics, annotations, and synchronous feedback are increasingly frequent methods used among those in evaluation and supervisory roles. Technology through portfolios and formal evaluation systems are common, formal mechanisms for documenting teachers' performance.

Portfolios

Performance-based assessments, via portfolios, include authentic demonstrations of skills and teaching abilities within the contexts of classrooms and schools (Wiggins, 1989). Historically, portfolios served as an evaluation tool, a format for reflection, and a tool that allowed mentors and supervisors to guide teachers as they documented their professional repertoires. In these early days of documenting practice, the content of these performance assessments was relatively nuanced, individualized, and "home grown" (Sato, 2014). Technological advances in documenting teaching quality situate electronic portfolios as both the receptacles

78 *Technology Integration in Supervision*

of more traditional artifacts of practice (e.g., lesson plans) and video demonstrations of practice (Castle & Shaklee, 2006; Wise et al., 2008; Coggshall et al., 2008).

An organization that adopted the portfolio model is the National Board for Professional Teaching Standards (NBPTS). The NBPTS served as the first professional organization responsible for acknowledging teaching excellence in formalized ways. A central feature of National Board Certification criteria includes teachers' reflections on select artifacts that demonstrate compliance with teaching competency indicators (DOE, 2016).

Early NBPTS formats included the development of paper portfolios, and later, online portfolios where the content includes the compilation of artifacts that aligns with various standards (e.g., curriculum, pedagogy, assessment). Performance assessments such as edTPA (Parkes & Powell, 2015) incorporate explicit, standardized evaluation systems for reviewing teaching where established rubrics are used to rate teaching snapshots.

For teacher educators at the preservice and in-service levels, adherence to performance assessment measures requires vigilance in supervisory support that aligns with the rigor and support parameters of evaluation, while simultaneously adhering to programmatic goals that are rooted in the relationships with students, families, colleagues, and communities (Sato, 2014; Schulte, 2012). For supervisors, performance assessments offer a starting place for evaluation frameworks that guide practices through programmatic structures (e.g., curriculum, pedagogy, assessment). While these structures are important, supervisors are encouraged to support ownership and agency among their teachers because compliance with standardized measures of performance may be a distraction from the reflection potential (Ledwell & Oyler, 2016). As such, supervisors are encouraged to support teachers' thinking beyond narrow profiles of performance that are sometimes scripted within electronic formats.

Video Storytelling and Case Studies: Tools for E-Supervision and Mentoring

On the surface, video-taped episodes of teaching offer a way to revisit teaching from a new vantage point. Videos encourage "storytelling" where supervisors examine teaching through narratives and perceptions of teaching events (Alger & Kopcha, 2009). Perspective allows supervisors to guide teachers as they relive the lesson in specific ways. Pinpointing dimensions of curriculum and instruction pushes teachers and supervisors to explore the nuances of teaching when video segments are used as lessons of study (Llinares & Valls, 2007). Supervisors assist teachers in making sense of teaching when they are prompted to identify how knowledge is embedded within contexts.

Building perspectives includes guiding teachers in their interpretations, naming, describing, and noticing what is happening during teaching episodes. Fostering this approach moves beyond more common analyses of teaching that are prescriptive and technocratic (Llinares & Valls, 2007). This "meaning making" aligns with the proposal shared earlier in discussions where communities of practice are fostered (Wegner et al., 2002). For example, Llinares and Valls (2007) suggest using videos and language analyses where individual teachers and groups share feedback for specific lessons. Their focus on knowledge building and "meaning making" among preservice teachers and their mentors created electronic spaces for mentors to examine and interpret teaching. By revisiting focal areas mentors encouraged teacher thinking, beyond technical skill.

Advanced-level analyses of lessons through reviews of teaching episodes allow for higher-level thinking, reflection, and attention to the range of factors that impact teaching and learning (Llinares & Valls, 2007). The prompts, challenges, and questions of supervisors were particularly critical in that they helped shape specific areas "noticed" by preservice teachers. The combination of the specific content of mathematics classrooms in this study, partnered with public discourse across themes that were tracked through electronic discussion "chains," encouraged greater depth in thinking about mathematics teaching (Llinares & Valls, 2007).

The process of understanding the role of contexts in classrooms underscores the work of teachers who work in tandem with mentors to examine teaching as more than skill building, thereby strengthening reflection on practice, their knowledge base, and ultimately, their agency as professionals. Supervisors that address depth and critical thinking prompt a professional stance that emboldens their agency in professional decision-making and models for teachers the value of depth in content knowledge and the importance of reflection on practice.

Conclusion

Today's education communities face the sometimes competing goals of improving teachers' work through support geared toward personal and professional growth while managing mandates for oversight and evaluation. For supervisors, facilitating teacher development is enhanced by taking advantage of a range of resources. Technology integration in mentoring and supervisory support holds the potential to enhance ownership and agency in classroom teaching by fostering authority for teachers and their supervisors as part of a larger community of professional decision makers.

References

Alger, C., & Kopcha, T. (2009). eSupervision: A technology framework for the 21st century field experience in teacher education. *Issues in Teacher Education*, *18*(2), 31–46.

80 Technology Integration in Supervision

Alliance for Excellent Education. (2004). *Tapping the potential: Retaining and developing new high-quality teachers*. Washington, DC: Author.

Aragon, A., & Kaminski, K. (2012). Racist Facebook event against Native Americans: Preservice teachers explore ethical and critical multiracial implications. *i-manager's Journal of Educational Technology, 9*(1), 35.

Alvarez, I., Espasa, A., & Guasch, T. (2011). The value of feedback in improving collaborative writing assignments in an online learning environment. *Studies in Higher Education, 37*(4), 387–400. doi:10.1080/03075079.2010.510182

Bagley, E. A., & Shaffer, D. W. (2015). Stop talking and type: Comparing virtual and face-to- face Mentoring in epistemic game. *Journal of Computer Assisted Learning, 31*(6), 606–622.

Benko, S., Guise, M., Earl, C., & Gill, W. (2016). More than media: Using Twitter with preservice teachers as a means of reflection and engagement in communities of practice. *Contemporary Issues in Technology and Teacher Education (CITE Journal), 16*(1), 1–21.

Berry, B. (2007). *Supporting new teachers: Considerations for virtual mentoring.* Carrboro, NC: Center for Teaching Quality.

Berry, B., & Nussbaum-Beach, S. (2006*). Personal communication with teachers for a new era.* Carrboro, NC: Center for Teaching Quality.

Bierema, L., & Hill, J. R. (2005). Virtual mentoring and HRD. *Advances in Developing Human Resources, 7*(5), 556–568.

Bonnel, W., & Boehm, H. (2011). Improving feedback to students online: Teaching tips from experienced faculty. *The Journal of Continuing Education in Nursing, 42*(11), 503–509. http://dx.doi.org/10.3928/00220124-20110715-02

Brown, M., Higgins, K., & Hartley, K. (2001). Teachers and technology equity. *Teaching Exceptional Children, 33*(4), 32–39.

Burbank, M. D., Ramirez, L., & Bates, A. J. (2016). The impact of critical reflective teaching: A rhetoric continuum. *Action in Teacher Education, 38*(2), 104–119.

Callahan, C., Saye, J., & Brush, T. (2015). Supporting in-service teachers' professional teaching knowledge with educatively scaffolded digital curriculum. *Contemporary Issues in Technology and Teacher Education, 15*(4), 568–599.

Castle, S., & Shaklee, B. D. (Eds.). (2006). *Assessing teacher performance: Performance-based assessment in teacher education.* Lanham, MD: Rowman & Littlefield Education.

Charbonneau-Gowdy, P., Capredoni, R., Gonzalez, S., Jayo, J., & Raby, P. (2016). Brave forms of mentoring and supervision supported by technology in teacher education. *The Electronic Journal of e-Learning, 14,* 3–14.

Christopherson, K. (2007). The positive and negative implications of anonymity in Internet social interactions: "On the internet, nobody knows you're a dog". *Computers in Human Behavior, 23,* 3038–3056.

Coffey, B., & Woolworth, S. (2004). Destroy the scum and then neuter their families: The web forum as a vehicle for community discourse? *The Social Science Journal, 41,* 1–14.

Coggshall, J., Max, J., & Bassett, K. (2008, June). *Key issue: Using performance-based assessment to identify and support high-quality teachers.* Washington, DC: National Comprehensive Center for Teacher Quality. Retrieved from www.tqsource.org

Technology Integration in Supervision 81

Cornelius, S., Gordon, C., & Harris, M. (2011). Role engagement and anonymity in synchronous online role play. *International Review of Research in Open and Distance Learning, 12,* 57–73.

Council for the Accreditation of Educator Preparation (CAEP). (2017). Retrieved from http://caepnet.org

Curran, M. (2014). Teacher candidates and twitter: Learning with iMentors. *Academic Exchange Quarterly, 18*(3).

Darling-Hammond, L., & Snyder, J. (2000). Authentic assessment of teaching in context. *Teaching and Teacher Education, 16*(5–6), 523–545.

Downes, S. (2009, October 5). Origins of the term "personal learning network" [blog post]. *Half an Hour.* Retrieved from http://halfanhour.blogspot.com/2009/10/origins-of-term-personal-learning.html

Doyle, P. (2015). *Twitter and professional development for teachers.* Retrieved from https://umanitoba.ca/faculties/education/media/2015-Doyle-Paul.pdf

Florell, D. (2016). Web-based training and supervision. In J. Luiselli & A. Fischer (Eds.), *Computer-assisted and web-based innovations in psychology, special education, and health* (pp. 313–337). San Francisco, CA: Elsevier.

Gallant, J. P, & Thyer, B. (2008). The "bug-in-the-ear" in clinical supervision. *The Clinical Supervisor, 7*(2–3), 43–58.

Gareis, C. G., & Nussbaum-Beach, S. L. (2007). Electronic mentoring to develop accomplished professional teachers. *Journal of Personnel Evaluation in Education, 20,* 227–246.

Gilbert, S. (2016). Learning in a Twitter-based community of practice: An exploration of knowledge exchange as a motivation for participation in #hcsmca. *Information, Communication, & Society, 19*(9), 1214–1232. doi:10.1080/13 69118X.2016.1186715

Hawkes, M., & Rosmiszowski, A. (2001). Examining the reflective outcomes of asynchronous computer-mediated communication on in-service teacher development. *Journal of Technology and Teacher Education, 9*(2), 285–308.

Herrington, J., Herrington, A., Mantei, J., Olney, I., & Ferry, B. (2009). New technologies, new pedagogies: Using mobile technologies to develop new ways of teaching and learning. In J. Herrington, A. Herrington, J. Mantei, I. Olney, & B. Ferry (Eds.), *New technologies, new pedagogies: Mobile learning in higher education* (pp. 1–14). Wollongong, Australia: University of Wollongong. Retrieved from www.scribd.com/document/17089209/New-Technologies-New-Pedagogies-Project-Using-Mobile-Technologies-to-Develop-New-Ways-of-Teaching- and-Learning

Israel, M., Knowlton, E., Griswold, D., & Rowland, A. (2009). Applications of video- conferencing technology in special education preparation. *Journal of Special Education Technology, 24*(1), 15–25.

Jacobs, J., Hogarty, K., & Burns, R. W. (2017). Elementary preservice teacher field supervision: A survey of teacher education programs. *Action in Teacher Education, 39*(2), 172–186. doi:10.1080/01626620.2016.1248300

Jaffe, R., Moir, E., Swanson, E., & Wheeler, G. (2006). Online mentoring and professional development for new science teachers. In C. Dede (Ed.), *Online teacher professional development: Emerging models and methods* (pp. 89–116). Cambridge, MA: Harvard Education Press.

Jackson, P. (1990). *Life in classrooms.* New York, NY: Teacher College, Columbia University Press.

82 Technology Integration in Supervision

Jamison, K. A. (2004). *The effects of trained facilitation of learning-oriented feedback on learner engagement, performance, self-efficacy, and enjoyment* (Order No. 3241135, Virginia Polytechnic Institute and State University). ProQuest Dissertations and Theses, pp. 1–137.

Jervis, K. (1996). *Eyes on the child: Three portfolio stories.* New York, NY: National Center for Restructuring Education, Schools and Teaching.

Kapadia, K., & Coca, V., & Easton, J. (2007). *Keeping new teachers: A first look at the influences of induction in the Chicago public schools.* Chicago, IL: Consortium on Chicago School Research at the University of Chicago.

Lave, J., & Wenger, E. (1990). *Situated learning: Legitimate peripheral participation.* Cambridge: Cambridge University Press.

Ledwell, K., & Oyler, C. (2016). Unstandardized responses to a "standardized" test: The edTPA as gatekeeper and curriculum change agent. *Journal of Teacher Education, 67*(2), 120–134. doi:10.1177/0022487115624739

Leibold, N., & Schwarz, L. (2015). The art of giving online feedback. *The Journal of Effective Teaching, 15,* 34–46.

Llinares, S., & Valls, J. (2007). The building of pre-service primary teachers' knowledge of mathematics teaching: Interaction and online video case studies. *Instructional Science, 37*(3), 247–271. doi:10.1007/s11251-007-9043-4

Lortie, D. (2002). *Schoolteacher: A sociological study* (2nd ed.). Chicago, IL: University of Chicago Press.

Maheu, M. M., Pulier, M. L., McMenamin, J., & Posen, L. (2012). Future of telepsychology, tele-health, and various technologies in psychological research and practice. *Professional Psychology: Research and Practice, 43,* 613–621. doi:10.1037/a002945

Parkes, K. A., & Powell, S. R. (2015). Is the edTPA the right choice for evaluating teacher readiness? *Arts Education Policy Review, 16*(2), 103–113. doi:10.1090/10632913.2014.944964

Risser, H. (2013). Virtual induction: A novice teacher's use of Twitter to form an informal mentoring network. *Teaching and Teacher Education, 35,* 25–33.

Rousmaniere, T. (2014). Using technology to enhance clinical supervision and training. In C. E. Watkins & D. Milne (Eds.), *International handbook of clinical supervision* (pp. 204–237). New York, NY: Wiley Publishing.

Sato, M. (2014). What is the underlying conception of teaching of the edTPA? *Journal of Teacher Education, 65*(5), 421–434. doi:10.1177/0022487114542518

Scheurich, J., & Young, M. (1997). Coloring epistemologies: Are our research epistemologies racially biased? *Educational Researcher, 26*(4), 4–16.

Schulte, A. (2012, December 14). Ann Schulte: Teacher performance assessment isn't the answer (Living in Dialogue). *Education Week Teacher.* Retrieved from http://blogs.ed-week.org/teachers/living-in-dialogue/2012/12/ann_schulte_teacher_performanc.html

Smith, S. J., & Israel, M. (2010). E-mentoring: Enhancing special education teacher induction. *Journal of Special Education Leadership, 23*(1), 30–40.

Todd, G. (2012). Talking beats writing. *Educational Leadership, 70*(1), 90.

US Department of Education. (2016). *Standards, assessment, and accountability.* www2.ed.gov/admins/lead/account/saa.html

Wegner, E., McDermott, R., & Snyder, W. M. (2002). *Cultivating communities of practice: Guide to managing knowledge.* Boston, MA: Harvard Business School.

Wei, R. C., & Pechone, R. (2010). Assessment for learning in preservice teacher education. In M. M. Kennedy (Ed.), *Teacher assessment and quality for teacher quality: A handbook*. San Francisco, CA: Jossey-Bass.

Wiggins, G. (1989). A true test: Toward more authentic and equitable assessment. *Phi Delta Kappan, 70*(9), 703–713.

Wise, A. E., Ehrenberg, P., & Leibbrand, J. (Eds.). (2008). *It's all about student learning: Assessing teacher candidates' ability to impact P-12 students*. Washington, DC: National Council for the Accreditation of Teacher Education.

5 Leadership and Professional Development

Beginning and early career educators' time and energy are often consumed with managing the logistics and related demands of teachers' work. Attention to the preparation and delivery of lessons as well as interacting with dozens to hundreds of students (at the secondary level) leaves many educators with limited time to consider their own professional development. Like teachers, mentors may experience the limitations of time as they shepherd new educators in a climate that is increasingly demanding for those working in P–12 classrooms.

Because mentors have a unique role, they must be provided adequate training and professional development necessary to serve in their assigned positions (Mumford, Campion, & Morgeson, 2007; Mumford, Marks, Connelly, Zaccaro, & Reiter-Palmon, 2000). We cannot assume mentors automatically possess leadership skills or the knowledge of how to address the impact of contexts and school cultures.

This chapter considers professional development and leadership experiences for mentors in the support they provide for others as well as their individual advancement. We explore the roles of educational contexts, emerging opportunities for leadership among mentors, and experiences that allow supervisors to foster agency among the educators with whom they work. Understanding leadership opportunities not only strengthens supervisory practices but fuels ownership and agency in defining the workplace trajectory for these supervisors in their roles as education professionals.

Creating Effective Supervisors as School Leaders

As education communities are aware, recruiting into teaching remains a priority for teacher preparation programs, districts, and states. Employment trends over the past 10 years underscore a pattern where between 40% and 50% of those who enter the profession continue to leave within the first 5 years (American Association of Colleges of Teacher Education [AACTE], 2018; Aragon, 2016; Ingersoll & Strong, 2011; Rich, 2015). Further complicating responses to teacher shortages are preparation

Leadership and Professional Development 85

efforts with mixed results, including variance in program quality, retention outcomes among graduates, and impact on diverse communities (Helig & Jez, 2010; Laczko-Kerr & Berliner, 2002; Sas, 2014). Suffice it to say, teacher shortages and attrition burden districts and schools through the costs incurred, limited experience within the workforce, and a paucity of informed leaders. Of greater significance is the impact on P–12 student learning and the long-term sustainability of the teaching profession (Alliance for Excellent Education, 2014; Clotfelter, Ladd, & Vigdor, 2006; Rice, 2010). In response to the need for more teachers a range of options in preparation have emerged.

Changes in the profile of teacher preparation highlight the importance of dedicated supervision and mentoring for preservice and beginning teachers. Chapter 1 of this book outlined an emerging trend of quick turnaround pathways to licensure (e.g., alternative routes to licensure) in teacher preparation and the differences in program types where mentoring and supervisory support are particularly critical. Currently, 12% of candidates are prepared through routes other than traditional university teacher preparation programs (AACTE, 2018). Regardless of preparation emphases for preservice and novice teachers, supervisors must ensure that those entering classrooms receive adequate and sustained support as they gain professional competencies (Sas, 2014).

Those assigned to support educators often find themselves in unplanned leadership positions as districts and schools scramble to build in mentoring and evaluation systems for teachers (Sas, 2014). At issue is whether supervisors are provided with the structures and related support necessary for navigating the evaluation systems in place.

In addition to providing general mentoring and problem-solving, the work of teacher leaders often includes areas such as evaluating performance, curriculum development, and instructional training (i.e., content and instructional coaching). Furthering the complexity of this work are the contexts of schools and classrooms. The existing cultures, norms, and expectations for educators require dedicated attention by many, including teacher leaders, to ensure professional longevity for members of teaching communities.

In response to the increase in preparation options for teachers, districts may employ teacher specialists whose paid assignments provide collegial support for professional development and retention. Mentoring is also provided by teachers within a designated school who are appointed as supervisory colleagues in less formal ways. Typically, these positions include assignments where teachers support the transition of colleagues into the profession or within a new school (DeCesare, Workman, & McClelland, 2016). For the most part, these positions are unpaid, and are in addition to full time teaching responsibilities. More formalized roles for teacher mentoring take place with varying levels of training, compensation, and opportunities for advancement within districts. The

86 *Leadership and Professional Development*

varied expectations for district and building-level supervisors and mentors underscores the need for dedicated attention to cultivating leadership roles in ways not considered in the past.

Supervisors as Change Agents Through the Facilitation of Teacher Leadership

As educational leaders, supervisors are in the position to promote individual agency for their mentees through guidance and posing problems as a catalyst for informed practice and decision-making. Simultaneously, engagement in this work also impacts supervisors and mentors through opportunities to advance their own leadership potential (Lumpkin, Claxton, & Wilson, 2014; Trybus, 2011). It is the power of leadership, as a dimension of agency among supervisors, which elevates the work of these professionals by advancing their professional growth opportunities. In theory, these goals make sense. In practice, the roles of contexts and the profession shape the ways in which leadership unfolds.

On a grand scale, media depictions of teacher leaders sometimes highlight sensationalized vignettes of teachers, portrayed as exceptional in their actions (Matthews, 1988; Gruwell, 2007). For example, a review of the work of urban educator Erin Gruwell (2007), showcases how she, like many other educators (e.g., Jaime Escalante) engage in sometimes superhuman activities to teach and lead students from peril. Through her story of leadership, others are likely inspired and motivated to envision possibilities for students' learning in ways that impact systems change (Morgan & Lock, 2014). While she is atypical in the depths of her actions, she demonstrates the potential in all educators to impact change, thereby advancing teacher agency as part of their classroom and school communities (Ackerman & MacKenzie, 2006). The common thread across these leadership profiles is their engagement in actions that impact educational systems (Morgan & Lock, 2014). Though for most educators, these actions don't take place in isolation without the influence of colleagues. Mentors have a unique contribution to these efforts.

As a community, educators possess the personal and professional qualities to inform effective leadership both in their classrooms and beyond. However, it is the specialized role of mentors that underscores their ability to tap into the potential of the educators with whom they work. As change agents within classrooms and schools, mentors are uniquely positioned to influence novice educators to cultivate skills and ways of thinking that can strengthen their leadership potential across the P–12 spectrum (Trybus, 2011). In these ways, mentors are poised to communicate a vision for professional advancement by empowering others within school communities.

Varied Roles

In their roles, mentors find themselves in the unique position of assuming the role of insider and outsider within education communities. Supervisors come with classroom experience, are familiar with the cultures of classrooms and schools, and are able to recognize operational realities within these settings. In these ways they are true insiders. For those who assume more formal mentoring and supervisory positions within higher education or within districts, opportunities for leadership bring new responsibilities and venues for professional advancement. In these ways, they assume roles that distance them from the daily work of educators.

To understand how supervisors may transform and support changes in educator practice, it is important to recognize the ways supervisors share their knowledge and experiences across settings as they advance as leaders in the field. Practically, mentors may find themselves in the position of straddling two types of assignments. Because they are both formally and informally "raised" as professionals working in P–12 classrooms, moving from teachers of children to teachers of adults requires different skills as well as opportunities to assume positions of leadership.

Chapter 2 of this text outlined the unique role of mentors in their work with adults and the consideration of how supervisors' knowledge and experiences inform their capacity to guide mentees. Unique to their work with adults is creating a balance between skill development for beginning and novice teachers with efforts designed to advance teacher agency through in-depth examinations of practice. To this end, mentors may lead colleagues by guiding professional practices that increase ownership and decision making among P–12 teachers. As educational leaders, supervisors and mentors are in the position to foster agency through informed decision-making via reflection on practice and systematic reviews of teachers' work.

Practitioner Knowledge Matters

In their seminal work on the role of teachers' knowledge development and research on practice, *Inside/Outside: Teacher Research and Knowledge*, Cochran-Smith and Lytle (1993) discuss teachers' work as complex, impacted by contexts, and within their authority and leadership as professionals. The authors invite a perspective on teachers' reflection where teacher knowledge is manifest in many ways, including research informed by educators' daily work. Cochran-Smith and Lytle (1993) recognize educators' competencies as part of a wider knowledge base that acknowledges and values their contributions. By legitimizing what teachers bring to the table, efficacy and professional agency are fostered. Of equal significance are documented professional growth efforts that

88 Leadership and Professional Development

showcase tangible outcomes of success for educators. Among other tools, action research provides these opportunities.

As members of education communities, mentors have the potential to influence professional environments through decision-making that includes systematic reflection and examinations of data (Cochran-Smith & Lytle, 1993). In concert with peers, semiformal groups of educators may work with grade level or content area teams as a way of reflecting on teaching. These experiences create both problem-solving opportunities as well as platforms for conversation among learning communities (Cochran-Smith & Lytle, 1993; DuFour & Eaker, 1998; Hord, 2004; Senge, 1990, 2000; Wenger, McDermott, & Snyder, 2002).

Because effective community building does not happen on its own, deliberate action must be taken to nurture these goals. Features such as group structures, roles assumed by participants, and nuances of communication styles impact long-term viability and impact community-building efforts (Blankenship & Ruona, 2007). In their research, Blankenship and Ruona (2007) compared a series of professional learning community models through analyses of the theoretical framework, participants, leadership, organizational culture, and knowledge sharing. Unique to their examination was attention to the ways teachers contribute as part of community-based decision-making. Specifically, teachers who adopted leadership roles were positioned to encourage and facilitate lasting engagement in decision-making. This stance acknowledges both individual and group perspectives to influence organizational change. Through the direct guidance and facilitation of mentors, teachers are provided with the structures that Blankenship and Ruona (2007) suggest as necessary for successful communities of teachers in their roles as decision makers. We must also consider the nuances of leadership roles for those engaged in this work.

In their own right, these teacher teaming efforts bring educators together for professional decision-making but may be limited if solely focused on problem-solving. By infusing the roles of mentors with the responsibility to lead teachers within these contexts, opportunities are created to promote ongoing reflection and teacher-led initiatives toward systems change (Blankenship & Ruona, 2007; Hord, 2004).

Frameworks that allow teachers to review their work systematically, gather data, and collaborate with others create spaces for data-based decision-making as central to their work. Lumpkin et al. (2014) and DeCesare et al. (2016) highlight the range of leadership roles that teachers might engage. Initial efforts may include involvement in peer support teams, observations and hybrid communication across sites, and training as content coaches or members of professional learning communities (PLCs) (Dufour & Eaker, 1998; Liston, Borko, & Whitcomb, 2008). Within each of these different roles, there are potential for changes in outcomes in practice and the development of improved school cultures

(Lambert, 2003). Additionally, engaging in these intentional professional development processes situates supervisors, as well as teachers, in experiences where they advance in dedicated leadership roles.

Dimensions of Educational Leadership

Research on the role of leadership in education reveals a range of factors impacting organizations including, but not limited to, leadership styles, leader efficacy, and strategy implementation (Hannah, Avolio, Luthans, & Harms, 2008; Marzano, Pikering, & Pollock, 2001). For those outside of the traditional leadership hierarchy, Harrison and Killion (2007) suggest a range of roles where educators' expertise inform classroom teaching and opportunities for site-based and community leadership.

Historically, school-based leadership has been assigned to principals and, to some extent, content-specific or general-area specialists. These individuals have been responsible for the daily operations, evaluation, and support services necessary to keep schools running. Current efforts to widen the leadership pool are designed to create platforms where teachers engage in leadership beyond the more typical operational responsibilities of building principals.

Informally, leadership roles for teachers may include providing resources for those they supervise as well as engaging as a co-learner in the process of improving teaching. On a practical level, informal leadership includes working with principals or other teachers holding advisory roles (Danielson, 2007; Killion & Harris, 2006). Formal leadership roles that are typically outside of the classroom teachers include instructional and curriculum coaches, mentors, school leaders, and data coaches (McCamish, Reynolds, Algozzine, & Cusumano, 2015). In each of these positions, teachers are afforded opportunities to assume new possibilities in their work or benefit from the support provided from those in supervisory roles. However, simply distributing job assignments does not guarantee proper training or opportunities for professional advancement. A systematic approach to mentor development requires a collective commitment to actions that build leadership potential that support long-term goals of advancing individual outcomes, increasing retention, and positively impacting student learning (Fletcher & Strong, 2009). Leadership communities are one step in this direction.

Ankrum (2016) cites the effort to build leadership cadres as a central goal of a school with buy-in from school stakeholders. Ankrum (2016) further outlines the mechanisms that create opportunities for teachers to assume positions in ways that are planned and supported. Within these school contexts, a mutual agreement between traditional leaders and classroom teachers assumes a willingness by teachers and their mentors to engage in varied leadership positions. In this way, the work is

90 *Leadership and Professional Development*

reciprocal and includes sharing responsibilities and influence. This process flattens what is typically seen as a hierarchical approach to governance. Further, individual and group participation in decision making and systems change encourages interdependence and agreement among participants (Leithwood et al., 2009). But what does this process look like?

Practically, an organizational leadership style that allows for greater sharing in decision-making and oversight creates a workplace where stakeholders are woven into operations and management. Distributed leadership (Heck & Hallinger, 2009) embodies a philosophy that embraces management and guidance and allows for equity in stakeholder engagement. Within contexts that allow for the distribution of leadership, mentors work collaboratively with teachers and principals to develop strategies nested in long-term goals of improving teaching and student learning. Engaging in this work requires a spirit of a collective investment toward common goals, ownership, and institutional betterment. This ethos, along with dedicated attention to skills and the acknowledgment of contexts, creates an opportunity to further the leadership potential of mentors.

Supervisors as Leaders: Skills and Dispositions

For educators who are committed to systems change, the critical need for defined opportunities to engage in this work must take place over time and on multiple levels (Lumpkin et al., 2014; Trybus, 2011). To enact this work, educators, and supervisors must be provided with settings that allow for role development as well as practical skill preparation to assume the responsibilities of work outside of traditional teaching.

The process of cultivating leadership is certainly personal. York-Barr and Duke (2004) highlight qualities of teachers that enhance their potential in areas including a history of demonstrated strengths in the classroom, dispositions that highlight an ability to work with others, and student success. These characteristics also apply to supervisors.

More fine-grained analyses identify the complexity of leadership roles and the factors that contribute to effectiveness (Day, Fleenor, Atwater, Sturm, & McKee, 2014). For example, variables including contexts, interpersonal experiences, skill development, and goals for advancement collectively impact how leadership may be enacted (Danielson, 2007; Day et al., 2014). As leaders themselves, supervisors must understand and address the layered dimensions of contexts that impact leadership success in their work to support teacher leaders.

Beyond the practical roles supervisors play in leadership (e.g., overseeing committees, evaluation), both small and large-scale contributions of mentors underscore their potential to influence systemic change (Ackerman & MacKenzie, 2006; Morgan & Lock, 2014). To this end, supervisors are in the position to serve as conduits for action and decision-making that inform teachers' work. In doing so, they have the capacity and the agency to impact how schools and classrooms operate both locally and beyond (Trybus, 2011).

Finally, in a study of five Midwestern U.S. states, 69% of new teachers received support from mentors whose primary roles were classroom teaching (DeCesare et al., 2016). For those in these mentoring positions, these more informal roles were in addition to their full-time assignments with no release from their teaching-related responsibilities. Slightly more than half of the mentors were required to observe their mentee's teaching, about a third received formal training, and slightly more than half received funding for their efforts (DeCesare et al., 2016). As with teachers, a practice of "volunteerism" pervades the mentoring profession in ways that assume educators' time is plentiful and remuneration unnecessary. For educators who seek to expand their influence, the routes are varied and complex. The role of "coach" is an assignment gaining prevalence within school communities in ways that highlight their expertise, autonomy, and leadership potential.

A Leadership Snapshot

A seminal model for enhancing teacher professional development through school-based mentoring support is captured in the classic work of Showers and Joyce (1996). Cognitive Coaching serves as a model for individualized, guided practice to improve teaching practice and student behavioral outcomes for strategy implementation (Snyder, Hemmeter, & Fox, 2015). Within the context of the coaching model, on-site teachers offer collegial support to improve teaching through problem identification, observational support and feedback, and long-term planning (McCamish et al., 2015). Over time, the Cognitive Coaching model expanded in explicit ways where teacher support became more focused to address content areas as well as classroom management as part of positive behavioral interventions and support (PBIS) (McCamish et al., 2015).

Outside of educational spheres, the concept of coaching is long-standing in the business community (Sherman & Freas, 2004). Job components include general communication skills, the ability to understand organizational cultures, and an ability to move through dimensions of work flexibly and quickly. Within school-based venues, coaching is conceptually described as a learning process (Gomez, 2016) and is particularly well aligned with the work of those engaged in mentoring as it relates to content area support.

Instructional Coaching

The role of instructional coaches (ICs) in educational contexts emerged formally in the early 2000s in response to efforts that required more

92   Leadership and Professional Development

formalized documentation of student performance and linkages to teacher performance. Analyses of student performance data prompted attention to areas of teachers' pedagogy in need of dedicated support. These needs were particularly noticeable as student performance data in mathematics and literacy were made public. Weaknesses in student performance intensified the focus of professional development for teachers through the support of coaches and mentors dedicated to building their skills as math and literacy teachers (Bean, 2004; Toll, 2005, 2007; Mraz, Salas, Mercado, & Dikotla, 2016).

Effective instructional coaching, supervision, or mentoring requires dedicated training. In addition to communication abilities, training must include attention to action planning, the development and enactment of growth plans, and evaluation of outcomes and impacts on individual and institutional change (Kee, Anderson, Dearing, Harris, & Shuster, 2010). Collectively these leadership skills are particularly relevant for supervisors working with both in-service teachers and preservice teachers.

A 2015 study by Farver and Holt further highlights the nuances necessary for effective coaching with a specific focus on the role of contexts in problem-solving. For the coaches in this study, self-confidence emerged when professionals engaged in thinking together in ways that aligned with their site-specific needs. In their roles, coaches recognized individuals, contexts, and group perspectives. This information informed their ability to create a supportive and trusting environment, maintain confidentiality, create opportunities for reflection, promote communication skill development, and create partnerships where colleagues think together. Finally, by establishing trusting relationships coaches created a setting that supported decision-making while simultaneously avoiding the isolation that is often a factor faced by those in leadership positions (Farver & Holt, 2015). This process of relationship building engenders agency and professional decision making among groups of educators.

Characteristics of Supervisors as Leaders

Data on perceptions of leadership styles reveal a range of characteristics related to decision-making, relationships between educational team members, and approaches to information sharing. Critical to these findings are the qualities of mentors that increase autonomy—independence and ownership in their work and in the skills they inform for others. The role of instructional coaches, as part of school-based leadership teams, is highlighted as unique as they supervise and mentor those under their direction.

A study by McCamish et al. (2015) documented self-reports of specific supervisory characteristics of coaches in their work as instructional coaches working in special education settings. The study's attention to the coaches' beliefs regarding their leadership styles offers a glimpse into an area that is typically missing in the research on educator support roles;

that is, self-reflections as well as documented time engaged in leadership roles are features of supervisory and mentoring that inform both mentor–mentee interactions and also serve to cultivate professional cultures that engender collaboration and community building.

For the participants in this study, self-report survey data identified differences across coaching styles and individuals' perceptions of overall effectiveness in providing support and networking (McCamish et al., 2015). Successful coaches reported a willingness to engage in leadership with the district-level support through information sharing and teamwork. Similar to content-based instructional coaches, these coaches reported higher engagement when they were provided with support, opportunities for relationship building, and goals for broad-based outcomes that went beyond simple skill development to include more conceptual components toward systems change.

Unique dimensions of the McCamish et al. (2015) study identified differences among leaders and their reported abilities to encourage what the authors describe as "transformational" approaches to supporting their colleagues. Unlike coaches who engaged in more punitive (i.e., transactional) or indecisive (i.e., laissez-faire) styles, coaches who embodied a transformational approach made relationship building and role-modeling central to their mentoring efforts. They reported greater success in encouraging teachers' growth and skill development (McCamish et al., 2015). Study findings are particularly relevant for mentors working with educators from across the developmental continuum. Specifically, leadership styles that employ transformational practices are nuanced in deliberate ways. Practices include inclusive participation through teacher-led goal setting that aligns with individual settings, and incorporate prioritized relationships among team members that extended beyond self-interest.

It is perhaps the agency that results from a transformational approach to coaching and mentoring that is among the most significant outcomes of this method. Leaders who engaged in transformational practices adopted a leadership style where teachers developed a greater sense of power, confidence, and a communal commitment to improving their teaching. These factors are critical features of systems change and have the potential to increase agency for both teachers and supervisors through empowerment and ownership in professional decision-making.

Building Capacity and Developing Potential for Supervision as Leadership

The work of supervisors with preservice teachers has a unique set of parameters. An inherent element of supervision includes mentoring to inform beginning teachers' skill development, knowledge of classrooms, and an understanding of learner differences that aligns with the assessment and curriculum demands of daily teaching. However, to expand the

94 *Leadership and Professional Development*

supervisor role as educational leaders and to instill leadership potential for the teachers with whom they work, both goal setting and a framework for operations are essential. Lessons from past models provide the technical skills for working as part of mentoring teams as well as a framework for developing leadership potential. The work of instructional coaches highlights those in mentoring positions who serve as leaders in support of beginning teachers.

An example of the impact of instructional coaches may be seen in an urban school district where educators receive tiered support as a means of developing and enhancing their ability to improve student learning outcomes (Granite School District, 2018). The training these coaches receive showcases how a commitment to teacher support through dedicated mentoring provides a foundation for leadership among cadres of educators. For these particular district instructional coaches, leadership responsibilities allow coaches to dive deeper into specializations and expertise as part of a multitiered system of teacher support. Over time and across settings, this framework allows for mentoring and guidance for coaches, nurtures individual growth among teachers, and advances leadership opportunities for those working in coaching positions. Central to this effort is a multilayered system of training.

First-year training for district coaches includes a review and reflection on Marzano and Simms's (2013) *Coaching Classroom Instruction* and Knight's (2007) *Instructional Coaching: A Partnership Approach to Improving Instruction* to guide general communication skills and approaches to mentoring. Under the direction of a district-appointed mentor, the first year of coaching training is designed to develop a deeper understanding of effective instruction and recommendations on how to assist novices in their development as beginning teachers. The training provided to coaches includes an overview of the coaching process and highlights their membership within school contexts.

Coaches in their second year study *Unmistakable Impact: A Partnership Approach for Dramatically Improving Instruction* (Knight, 2011) and *Quality Teaching in a Culture of Coaching* (Barkley, 2010). It is during their second year that coaches are transitioned from a standalone coach to memberships in collaborative partnership with other coaches. As a team, these educational leaders examine authentic ways to support each teacher at their current level of professional growth.

Instructional coaches entering their third year study *The Art of Coaching: Effective Strategies for School Transformation* (Aguilar, 2013). This is a more progressive approach to coaching where coaches are encouraged to entertain perspectives beyond their own pedagogical stance. Conversations and problem-solving center around issues in teaching that extend beyond instructional delivery that acknowledges contextual influences. A clear benefit of this process is that it allows coaches, as instructional leaders, to consider the range of factors that impact teaching and

Leadership and Professional Development   95

learning. In doing so, their impact as change agents both within their classrooms and school is enhanced.

Finally, during years four and five, third-year coaches who complete the training transition to administrative positions with the understanding that their experiences as coaches have provided opportunities to move into effective school leadership positions with an increased knowledge of teachers, contexts, and broad-based goals for education. This leadership advancement does not always mean leaving the classroom, though there are educators who may pursue that option. The key for fostering agency is providing educators, across positions, with the knowledge and experiences that build upon one another in ways that empower educators to understand their leadership roles as part of a systemic change.

Conclusion

The teaching profession is often described as a lonely endeavor (Flinders, 1988; Lortie, 2002). Similarly, those separated from daily work in classrooms such as supervisors, mentors, and administrators find themselves in positions of isolation and abandonment. These characteristics of "oneness" can be mainstays even in environments filled with hundreds and hundreds of people (Lortie, 2002; Ostovar-Nameghi & Sheikhahmadi, 2016). By working in teams and promoting collaborative decision-making, education professionals create spaces that counter the more commonplace limitations for collaboration and idea exchanges. Supervisors play essential roles in leading, guiding, bridging, and opening communication both for themselves and those who they influence.

Districts and schools have crafted efforts to support educators in order to combat the realities of teachers' work as insular and professionally sequestered. In addition to bolstering teaching, environments must be created to foster defined leadership and professional development experiences that provide structures for informal and formal dialogue. More recently, supervisors and coaches play a unique role in advancing areas including skill development and creating opportunities for individual leadership and efficacy in how educators execute their professional lives. Extant practices across many districts and schools provide formalized structures that allow educators to work as part of teams dedicated to programmatic and systems change. For example, memberships in professional learning communities (PLCs) (DuFour & Eaker, 1998) and related communities of practice offer educators structured and semi-structured experiences for thinking with others about actions in demonstrable ways.

Supervisory leadership within educational circles takes many forms. Support provided to preservice teachers and those beginning their careers offers both the skills as well as professional venues for collective decision-making among communities of practice. It is through the power of communities committed to educational change that agency is enhanced.

96 Leadership and Professional Development

It is the dedicated work of supervisors that creates opportunities for educators. Central to the work of leadership by those who mentor are the skills and dispositions necessary to transform practice. These efforts are critical to understand of the complexity of school contexts, the cultures of education on both micro and macro levels, and systemic structures that create opportunities for sustained and supportive dialogue (Berliner-Gustafson, 2004; DuFour & Eaker, 1998; Senge, 2000).

References

Ackerman, R., & Mackenzie, S. (2006). Uncovering teacher leadership. *Educational Leadership*, *63*, 66–70.

Aguilar, E. (2013). *The art of coaching: Effective strategies for school transformation*. San Francisco, CA: Josey-Bass.

Alliance for Excellent Education. (2014). *On the path to equity: Improving the effectiveness of beginning teachers*. Washington, DC: Author. Retrieved November 3, 2015, from http://all4ed.org/reports-factsheets/path-to-equity

American Association of Colleges of Teacher Education. (2018). *Colleges of education: A national portrait*. Washington, DC: Author.

Ankrum, R. (2016). Utilizing teacher leadership as a catalyst for change in schools. *Journal of Educational Issues*, *2*(1), 151–165.

Aragon, S. (2016). *Teacher shortages: What we know*. Education Commission of the States. Retrieved from www.ecs.org/ec-content/uploads/Teacher-Shortages-What-We-Know.pdf

Barkley, S. (2010). *Quality teaching in a culture of coaching* (2nd ed.). Lanham, MD: Rowman & Littlefield Education.

Bean, R. M. (2004). Promoting effective literacy instruction: The challenge for literacy coaches. *The California Reader*, *37*(3), 58–63.

Berliner-Gustafson, C. (2004, May). *Building professional learning communities*. Paper presented at the Support of the Florida Professional Development System Evaluation Protocol, FL.

Blankenship, S., & Ruona, W. (2007, February/March). *Professional learning communities and communities of practice: A comparison of models, literature review*. Online Submission. Paper presented at the Academy of Human Resource Development International Research Conference in The Americas, Indianapolis, IN.

Clotfelter, C., Ladd, H., & Vigdor, J. (2006). *Teacher-student matching and the assessment of teacher effectiveness*. Cambridge, MA: National Bureau of Economic Research. Retrieved from http://eric.ed.gov/?id=EJ750956

Cochran-Smith, M., & Lytle, S. (1993). *Inside/outside: Teacher research and knowledge*. New York, NY: Teachers College Press.

Danielson, C. (2007). The many faces of teacher leadership. *Educational Leadership*, *65*(1), 14–19.

Day, D., Fleenor, J., Atwater, L., Sturm, R., & McKee, R. (2014). Advances in leader and leadership development: A review of 25 years of research and theory. *The Leadership Quarterly*, *25*(1), 63–82.

DeCesare, D., Workman, S., & McClelland, A. (2016). *How do school districts mentor new teachers?* National Center for Education Evaluation and Regional

Leadership and Professional Development 97

Assistance. Institute of Education Sciences. Washington, DC: U.S. Department of Education.

DuFour, R., & Eaker, R. (1998). *Professional learning communities at work: Best practices for enhancing student achievement.* National Educational Service. Bloomington, IN: Solution Tree.

Farver, A., & Holt, C. (2015). Value of coaching in building leadership capacity of principals in urban schools. *Education Leadership Review of Doctoral Research, 2*(2), 67–76.

Fletcher, S. H., & Strong, M. (2009). Full-release and site-based mentoring of elementary grade new teachers: An analysis of changes in student achievement. *New Educator, 5*(4), 329–341.

Flinders, D. (1988). Teacher isolation and the new reform. *Journal of Curriculum and Supervision, 4*(1), 17–29.

Gomez, J. (2016). Instructional coaching implementation: Considerations for K-12 administrators. *Journal of School Administration Research and Development, 1*(2), 37–40.

Granite School District. (2018). *Teacher induction and support.* Retrieved from www.graniteschools.org/inductionintervention/

Gruwell, E. (2007). *Teach with your heart: Lessons I learned from the freedom writers.* New York, NY: Broadway Press.

Hannah, S., Avolio, B., Luthans, F., & Harms, P. D. (2008). Leadership efficacy: Review and future directions. *The Leadership Quarterly, 9*(6), 669–692. doi:10.1016/j.leaqua.2008.09.007

Harrison, C., & Killion, J. (2007). Ten roles for teacher leaders. *Educational Leadership, 65*(1), 74–77.

Heck, R. H., & Hallinger, P. (2009). Assessing the contribution of distributed leadership to school improvement and growth in math achievement. *American Educational Research Journal, 46*, 659–689.

Helig, J. V., & Jez, S. J. (2010). *Teach for America: A review of the evidence.* East Lansing, MI: Great Lakes Center for Education Research and Practice.

Hord, S. M. (2004). Professional learning communities: An overview. In S. Hord (Ed.), *Learning together, leading together: Changing schools through professional learning communities* (pp. 5–14). New York, NY: Teachers College Press.

Ingersoll, R., & Strong, M. (2011). The impact of induction and mentoring programs for beginning teachers: A critical review of the research. *Review of Educational Research, 81*(2), 201–233.

Kee, K., Anderson, K., Dearing, V., Harris, E., & Shuster, F. (2010). *Results coaching the new essential for school leaders.* Thousand Oaks, CA: Corwin Press.

Killion, J., & Harrison, C. (2006). *Taking the lead: New roles for teachers and school based coaches.* Oxford, OH: National Staff Development Council.

Knight, J. (2011). *Unmistakable impact: A partnership approach for dramatically improving instruction.* Thousand Oaks, CA: Corwin Press.

Knight, J. (2007). *Instructional coaching: A partnership approach to improving instruction.* Thousand Oaks, CA: Corwin Press.

Laczko-Kerr, I., & Berliner, D. (2002). The effectiveness of Teach for America and other under-certified teachers on student academic achievement: A case of harmful public policy. *Educational Policy Analysis Archives, 10*(37). Retrieved from http://epaa.asu.edu/epaa/v10n37

98 *Leadership and Professional Development*

Lambert, L. (2003). Leadership redefined: An evocative context for teacher leadership. *School Leadership & Management, 23*, 421–430.

Leithwood, K., Mascall, B., Strauss, T., Sacks, R., Memon, N., & Yashkina, A. (2009). Distributing leadership to make schools smarter: Taking the ego out of the system. *Leadership and Policy in Schools, 6*(1), 37–67.

Liston, D., Borko, H., & Whitcomb, J. (2008). The teacher educator's role in enhancing teacher quality. *Journal of Teacher Education, 59*(2), 111–116.

Lortie, D. C. (2002). *Schoolteacher: A sociological study* (2nd ed.). Chicago, IL: University of Chicago Press.

Lumpkin, A., Claxton, H., & Wilson, A. (2014). Key characteristics of teacher leaders in schools. *Administrative Issues Journal: Education, Practice, and Research, 4*(2), 59–67. doi:10.5929/2014.4.2.8

Marzano, R., & Simms, J. (2013). *Coaching classroom instruction.* Bloomington, IN: Marzano Research.

Marzano, R., Pikering, D., & Pollock, J. (2001). *Classroom instruction that works.* Alexandria, VA: Association for Supervision and Curriculum Development.

Matthews, J. (1988). *Jaime Escalante: The best teacher in America.* New York, NY: Henry Holt & Company.

McCamish, C., Reynolds, R., Algozzine, B., & Cusumano, D. (2015). An investigation of characteristics, practices, and leadership styles of PBIS coaches. *Journal of Applied Educational and Policy Research, 1*(1), 15–34.

Morgan, R., & Lock, P. (2014). Erin Gruwell: A biographical account of a teacher leader for change. *Educational Leadership and Administration: Teaching and Program Development, 25*, 65–76.

Mraz, M., Salas, S., Mercado, L., & Dikotla, M. (2016). Teaching better, together: Literacy coaching as collaborative professional development. *English Teaching Forum, 54*(2), 24–31.

Mumford, T. V., Campion, M. A., & Morgeson, F. P. (2007). The leadership skills strataplex: Leadership skill requirements across organizational levels. *The Leadership Quarterly, 18*(2), 154–166.

Mumford, M., Marks, M. A., Connelly, M. S., Zaccaro, S. J., & Reiter-Palmon, R. (2000). Development of leadership skills: Experience and timing. *The Leadership Quarterly, 11*(1), 87–114.

Ostovar-Nameghi, S., & Sheikhahmadi, M. (2016). From teacher isolation to teacher collaboration: Theoretical perspectives and empirical findings. *English Language Teaching, 9*(5), 197–205.

Rice, J. K. (2010). *The impact of teacher experience: Examining the evidence and policy implications.* Arlington, VA: National Center for Analysis of Longitudinal Data in Education Research. Retrieved from http://eric.ed.gov/?id=ED511988

Rich, M. (2015). Teacher shortages spur a nationwide hiring scramble (Credentials Optional). *New York Times.* Retrieved from www.nytimes.com/2015/08/10/us/teacher-shortages-spur-a-nationwide-hiring-scramble-credentials-optional.html?

Sas, T. (2014). *Licensure and worker quality: A comparison of alternative routes to teaching.* Atlanta, GA: Department of Economics W.J. Usery Workplace Research Group.

Senge, P. (2000). *Schools that learn: A fifth discipline fieldbook for parents, educators, and everyone who cares about education.* New York, NY: Doubleday.

Senge, P. M. (1990). *The fifth discipline: The art and practice of the learning organization*. New York, NY: Currency, Doubleday.

Sherman, S., & Freas, A. (2004). The Wild West of executive coaching. *Harvard Business Review, 82*(11), 82–90.

Showers, B., & Joyce, J. (1996). The evolution of peer coaching. *Educational Leadership, 53*(6), 1–5.

Snyder, P. A., Hemmeter, M. L., & Fox, L. (2015). Supporting implementation of evidence- based practices through practice-based coaching. *Topics in Early Childhood Special Education, 35*(3), 133–143.

Toll, C. A. (2005). *The literacy coach's survival guide: Essential questions and practical answers*. Newark, DE: International Reading Association.

Toll, C. A. (2007). *Lenses on literacy coaching: Conceptualizations, functions, and outcomes*. Norwood, MA: Christopher-Gordon.

Trybus, M. A. (2011). Facing the challenge of change: Steps to becoming an effective leader. *Delta Kappa Gamma Bulletin, 77*(3), 33–36.

Wenger, E., McDermott, R., & Snyder, W. M. (2002). *Cultivating communities of practice: A guide to managing knowledge*. Boston, MA: Harvard Business School.

York-Barr, J., & Duke, K. (2004). What do we know about teacher leadership? Findings from two decades of scholarship. *Review of Educational Research, 74*(3), 255–316.

6 Agency as a Means for Building Resilience

In today's schools, greater attention is paid to the issue of the trauma children experience, particularly given the potential and realized impact on student learning opportunities. As a result of this increased focus on student well-being, teachers are attending more to the development of resilience in children to equip them to better handle the complexities that are a part of their daily lives. Building resilience in children and young adults has become a cornerstone of many contemporary teachers' work.

The expectations for teachers are increasing when it comes to understanding the childhood trauma and toxic stress that manifest in the classroom. In response, educators must consider new ways to respond to not only the academic needs of students, but also the social and emotional needs of learners. Addressing each of these areas keeps classroom learning moving forward. As teachers acknowledge the realities of complex contemporary classrooms, there is also a collateral impact on the teachers with regard to their own self-care and the burdens of secondary stress, burnout, and compassion fatigue. As such, supervisors and mentors for early career teachers must be cognizant of the challenges those in the early stages of learning to teach face, given the high cognitive load that novices already experience in learning to respond productively in educational settings.

Acknowledging the social and emotional support role that a supervisor or mentor often plays will be a crucial part of understanding the complexity of the supervisory relationship. For the purposes of this text, we elected to use trauma as a conceptual example of the challenges that a teacher faces that weigh heavily on the heart and soul of teaching, and recognizing that trauma and stress are often topics addressed in more clinical terms—if at all—in teacher preparation programming. This chapter will look closely at the role that the supervisor plays in facilitating the development of resilience in the novice teacher, considering how the supervisor's agency to act serves both as a model for the novice and as a crucial part of ensuring that as much as possible is done to give the teacher the capacity and tools necessary to prosper or thrive through those first few difficult years of teaching. Additionally, the chapter will

Agency as a Means for Building Resilience 101

address the importance of building the resilience of supervisors and mentors as they work to meet the needs of novice teachers who are impacted by the experiences their students have with trauma and toxic stress.

What Are Trauma and Resilience?

Trauma is far more prevalent than previously understood and may have a significant, toxic impact on the development of the human brain (Burke Harris, 2018; Felitti et al., 1998; Souers & Hall, 2016). Trauma, defined as "an exceptional experience in which powerful and dangerous events overwhelm a persona' capacity to cope" (Rice & Groves, 2005, p. 3), enters the classroom as part of a child's (or teacher's) lived experience in the world that impacts physical, social, emotional, and psychological development (Burke Harris, 2018). The groundbreaking study in this area, conducted by Dr. Victor Felitti and colleagues, determined that childhood trauma has significant impacts on health outcomes throughout the life span. The adverse childhood experiences (ACEs) study looked closely at the impact of traumatic experiences in the areas of childhood abuse (emotional, physical and sexual), neglect (physical and emotional), and a series of household challenges (Center on the Developing Child [CDC], 2018). The experience of these traumatic events in childhood has shown increases over the life span in the following: "risky health behaviors, chronic health conditions, low life potential, and early death" (CDC, 2018). Nearly 60% of adults report experiencing trauma during childhood (National Center for Mental Health Promotion and Youth Violence Prevention, 2012). Physical problems are the lived manifestation of trauma on the human body and can impact learning through challenges that manifest themselves in the P–12 classroom (Burke Harris, 2018). While the impacts of trauma can be powerful on the body and the psyche, there are strategies that can be taught to children and families—as well as teachers—that can mediate these impacts (Burke Harris, 2018; O'Donnell, Schwab-Stone, & Muyeed, 2002; Souers & Hall, 2016).

When children learn resilience they develop the tools and capacity to withstand the impacts of trauma or rebound from them more quickly; they must be given the opportunity to spend time learning the skills and attitudes that will positively impact their development. As described by the Center on the Developing Child, "Resilience results from a dynamic interaction between internal predispositions and external experiences" (2015a, p. 1). There are several factors that can prepare students to deal with adverse experiences in a more positive fashion: "facilitating supportive adult–child relationships; building a sense of self-efficacy and perceived control; providing opportunities to strengthen adaptive skills and self-regulatory capacities; and mobilizing sources of faith, hope, and cultural traditions" (Center on the Developing Child Harvard University, 2018). The relationships between students and teachers have value in

102 *Agency as a Means for Building Resilience*

helping to build these bonds and foster resiliency in students (Souers & Hall, 2016).

It is crucial to note in the context of this work on agency in supervision, and the need for an effective mentoring relationship, that "resilience requires relationships, not rugged individualism." The Center on the Developing Child at Harvard University (2015b) notes that "it is the reliable presence of at least one supportive relationship and multiple opportunities for developing effective coping skills that are essential building blocks for the capacity to do well in the face of significant adversity" (Center on the Developing Child at Harvard University, 2015b, p. 7). While teachers have always held the responsibility of building meaningful relationships with students, increasingly, teachers are asked to develop relationships that move beyond effective learning and encompass a broader view of skills necessary for life success in all domains. Teachers serve as the visible face of support for many children in trauma, which requires them to regularly act on the information that children bring to the schools, resulting in the highest rate of referral for social services of any public service providers (VanBergeijk & Sarmiento, 2006).

Why Do Teachers Need to Be Highly Resilient?

Classroom environments can quickly become complicated working situations when the presence of trauma and toxic stress in children becomes a dominant factor in the daily interactions between children, their peers, and teachers. While it is necessary for teachers to create a resilience-enhancing, supportive relationship with each student in their classroom, it is also crucial that teachers have someone supporting them in a similar fashion (Abraham-Cook, 2012). The resilience of the teachers who support children experiencing or living with trauma is crucial to the long-term viability of their well-being, but also their ability and desire to stay in the profession and continue to meet the significant and demanding needs of their students. Much of this is done ad hoc—a teacher finds a colleague (other teacher, administrator, etc.) whom they trust to build these networks of support. However, there are teachers who struggle to find this connection, contexts that make it difficult to engage in this type of work, limitations on the time and space to prioritize this work, and so on. Finding support can also be a challenge to navigate for those who are new to the profession or to a school as they work to balance this need with the other intense demands on their time and energy. Relying on teachers to find this support for themselves rather than offering it as a part of mentoring or support resource provided to them is a burden that does not need to be borne solely by the teacher. It is incumbent on the profession to build these systems of support into practice such that all teachers are offered the tools they need to be successful with children and maintain their own resilience within the profession. Mentors and

Agency as a Means for Building Resilience   103

supervisors are in the position to be ones that play this support role and model for teachers how to continue to persevere in the face of these emotional burdens (Abraham-Cook, 2012; Stamm, 2002).

Impacts of Student Trauma on Teachers

The face of public education in the United States has transformed across many communities. Charter school movements and the status of the profession are among the shifts in how the profession is viewed. On the ground, teachers experience the pressures of both trends in the field as well as the lived challenges that are part of their daily work. These pressures are significant for educators who, as a group, have a reputation for putting themselves last, both personally and professionally. Given shifts in the climate of public education and the demands related to the nature of the profession (meeting the needs of a wide range of children each day) teachers find themselves in a challenging position.

As Souers and Hall (2016) describe:

> Our work in the caregiving fields is tremendously challenging and emotional. Our own self-care is imperative in helping us maintain our focus and avoid burnout—that point we reach when we've got nothing left to give, our tank is empty, and we have to exit the profession.
>
> (p. 194)

That said, the profound impact of secondary stress, burnout, and compassion fatigue can take a significant toll on teachers, particularly as it accumulates over the years of a career. "Working closely with a child who has experienced trauma exposes teachers and caregivers to that same trauma" (Lucas, 2007/2008, p. 86). These conditions result in a high rate of teacher turnover in the profession given the consequences on job satisfaction, personal mental and physical health, and impact on home life.

Teachers invest in the children in their care and work to develop the types of supportive teacher–student relationships that are conducive to building resilience in both parties. However, as each group of students comes and goes from the classroom, the cycle of attachment can weigh heavily on the teacher. Investing fully in children who are experiencing difficult traumas and working through those challenges, as teacher and student, takes a toll on the teacher given the emotional nature of the work done (Lucas, 2007/2008). Because teachers cannot exert control over each aspect of a child's life, when traumatic experiences are the cause of classroom issues, they often choose to leave the profession—feeling burned out from the lack of control and the complex cycle of engagement with children experiencing trauma.

Burnout

Educator burnout "is characterized along three dimensions that reflect feelings of job-related emotional exhaustion, depersonalization, and a sense of personal accomplishment" (Hoglund, Klingle, & Hosan, 2015, p. 338). Feelings of burnout can be exacerbated by the needs of children in schools with higher than average populations of students experiencing trauma (Pas, Bradshaw, & Hershfeldt, 2012), potentially resulting in lesser-quality instruction and negative relationships between students and teachers (Alvarez, 2007). Burnout, as a result of working with children experiencing trauma and evidencing significant needs for support, can become a vicious cycle between teachers and children when failing to interact in productive and meaningful ways that ensure quality instruction and useful, engaged relationships (Alvarez, 2007; Pas et al., 2012; Hoglund et al., 2015).

Compassion Fatigue and Secondary Traumatic Stress

Other challenges teachers address are compassion fatigue and secondary traumatic stress. Compassion fatigue is defined as "the range of adverse effects on caregivers due to their work with traumatized people" (Hamilton, 2008, p. 11) and may result in the inability to be emotionally available to oneself or others. Emotional distance from others and emotional numbness in stressful situations or in dealing with those who are in trauma are common symptoms of compassion fatigue (Figley, 2002). Secondary traumatic stress results from the exposure to the trauma experienced by others. For example, hearing the stories of the children in a teacher's class (Hamilton, 2008) can provide regular exposure to examples of the trauma students experience in their daily lives and can be viewed as synonymous with compassion fatigue (Abraham-Cook, 2012).

Abraham-Cook's (2012) study sample of urban public school teachers experienced high rates of compassion fatigue as compared to other mental health professionals, perhaps stemming from the daily, ongoing interactions that teachers have with students. A particularly concerning outcome for educators of compassion fatigue and secondary traumatic stress is the silencing response (Hamilton, 2008)—actively avoiding learning more about a situation in an attempt to avoid the required interaction or support outcomes necessary to move the student beyond the experience. While an understandable reaction by a teacher, it is one that cannot be ignored or avoided as it has negative consequences for both the teacher and the student who needs support in moving forward. Unlike burnout, which can be resolved by quitting one's job or making other drastic employment changes (moving to another school, for example), compassion fatigue and secondary traumatic stress are not situations that can be easily resolved.

Coping Mechanisms

It has become necessary to equip teachers with the tools for coping with this intensive experience and to ensure that educators possess the necessary skills for adult emotional regulation as they work to ensure that children are provided with safe and supportive learning environments. Two recommended coping mechanisms include reframing and realistic goal setting as strategies that support teachers in viewing the possible, potential, and positives in children (Lucas, 2007/2008; Bober, Regehr, & Zhou, 2006). Identifying positive outcomes of the relationships held with particular children and determining how teachers have made a difference for the student can also be reaffirming and work against fatigue (Hamilton, 2008; Tonder & Williams, 2009). Together, this research suggests that school and classroom work environments that are supportive and encouraging of teachers' abilities and confidence can ameliorate some of the impact of burnout over time (Abraham-Cook, 2012; Kahn, Schneider, Jenkins-Henkelman, & Moyle, 2006).

Finally, recommendations for supporting teachers include collaboration with mental health professionals (including school counselors and social workers) that can support teachers in identifying and responding to burnout and also in determining the best options for meeting the needs of children and families (Abraham-Cook, 2012; Alvarez, 2007; Hoglund et al., 2015; Hosan, Hoglund, & Richards, 2013). To ensure a safe beginning for all new teachers, "Secondary trauma and self-case strategies must be taught early in students' careers to ensure that they can anticipate and address their own reactions to the painful feelings evoked by their work" (Hamilton, 2008, p. 16). Building this capacity early on can have the effect of preparing teachers for the realities of the profession and their responsibilities to themselves as educators and individuals (Abraham-Cook, 2012), something that is beginning to emerge in teacher preparation programs.

Support for Supervisors and Mentors

Of crucial importance for educators in their work with children experiencing or who have experienced trauma is the impact on the mentor or supervisor when supporting the teachers. While the trauma of the students may not be as closely experienced or related to the mentor, there is the danger of responding to the compassion fatigue through the mentor's own lens. The mentor's previous personal and professional experiences may exacerbate the mentor's response. It is incumbent that the supervisor engage in the same recommended practices for the teacher as a means of developing and maintaining resilience in the face of the challenges present in the daily work of schools.

106 *Agency as a Means for Building Resilience*

Resilience and Agency

Educational systems, both school districts and educator preparation programs, must recognize the importance of developing structures that provide professional growth and support for teacher agency around trauma and resilience in classroom settings. Given the impact of their relationships and shared interactions on the daily life of the child, teachers must be supported as they work with children who have experienced trauma. Teachers have an ethical responsibility to do their best to fully engage in the work of teaching and learning without inadvertently causing harm to the children as a result of the secondary traumatic stress, compassion fatigue, or burnout of the teacher (Hamilton, 2008; Tonder & Williams, 2009).

Resilience development in teachers serves as a form of self-care as they work to ensure they are ready to greet the children each day with their best efforts. For example, research on school counselors and trauma may be mirrored with teachers as well. Like school counselors, educators who fail to care for themselves may serve as a very poor models for children of the effective ways to practice self-care and ensure the development of resilience over time (Monroe, 1995). Limited self-care can result in teachers who are more at risk for compassion fatigue and unable to balance their work–life load with the emotional needs of both themselves and their students (Abraham-Cook, 2012).

Compassion Satisfaction

Compassion satisfaction, the notion of the satisfaction that one gains from helping others, can serve as a positive outcome of the work teachers do with children who have experienced trauma (Abraham-Cook, 2012). Compassion satisfaction can work against teacher burnout and is in line with the coping strategies described earlier in the chapter. It also encourages teachers to see the positive outcomes they achieve with children and families that can reinvigorate them in the field (Abraham-Cook, 2012). Further, compassion satisfaction and compassion fatigue can coexist (Stamm, 2002), meaning that it is not necessary for educators to first do away with one in order to experience the other—a profound reminder for those working daily to succeed in high-intensity, sometimes traumatic environments. Learning how to balance the forces that impact teachers in these contexts is crucial to ensuring longevity in the profession. For supervisors, being clear about the responsibility that teachers have to themselves to attend to their well-being will be a support needed by many novice educators.

Agency

Similar to other recommendations to avoid the negative consequences of trauma and toxic stress, teacher agency is engaging in effective change for oneself and for the profession at large that can counteract compassion fatigue and burnout. A significant aspect of agency is the sense of control that can come with knowing when and how to act to effect change. Control is a defining feature in resilience, determining where it resides and learning how to manage the tensions between those areas where a teacher can exert control and where little authority may reside (e.g., being able to remove a child from a situation that causes extensive trauma or to quickly resolve the impact of trauma on a child). Lessons in agency learned and practiced can result in greater resilience with time and experience, something that novice educators lack by virtue of their time in the profession. According to Abraham-Cook (2012), "As younger teachers appear to be more vulnerable to the development of burnout, mentoring relationships between younger and more experienced educators may be of benefit" (p. 124). The concepts of supervisor agency that were developed throughout this text are a crucial part of the conversation about preparing teachers for success in contexts and relationships that include trauma.

Supervisors enact change by using their agency to support novice educators who are learning to become teachers in settings that are sometimes very challenging. Novice educators learn from experts about the areas of teaching that they can and cannot control, learning to develop their skill set of resilience-enhancing strategies and attitudes. Resilience and agency are related concepts in that both empower the educator to make and act on decisions that can impact teaching and learning, for educators and for children. Engaging in practice in this way reinforces the supportive communities and relationships that are designed to support compassion satisfaction rather than fatigue (Abraham-Cook, 2012). Continuing to be resilient about practice and support for children with traumatic experiences results in positive outcomes and compassion satisfaction thereby creating a deeper sense of resilience in beginning teachers. It is a cycle of reinforcement that can perpetuate success and growth on the part of the novice teacher. Using the supervisory role as a mentor of that cycle can result in the type of supportive relationships described above.

Resilience Leads to Agency

Over time, the more one practices the act of resilience, the more potential there is to be able to act on one's behalf (and others) to effect change. The development of resiliency can inform the sense of empowerment necessary to enact agency in the area of professional interest or growth meaningful to the supervisor or educator. Success in those first endeavors to assert agency (when the outcome is positive) can fuel the joy and power that keeps supervisors and mentors moving forward. In other words, resilience begets agency, which results in greater resilience, and the cycle continues. Feeling empowered to act and seeing the outcomes of that act

108 *Agency as a Means for Building Resilience*

in changing a situation or moment for another teacher, for a child, or for a classroom can result in powerful feelings of resilience—knowing that you have mental and emotional fortitude to keep going forward despite the bumps in the road that are inevitable. However, dwelling in the negative reduces agency by keeping one from acting in forward-growing ways, essentially giving away agency and power to act for change that would improve the situation. Throughout this work of using agency for change, it is important to realize that building resiliency is not an isolated proposition. It is inherently difficult to sustain the type of resilience and agency that are described here through engagement in change as an individual, without a team of support. As described earlier, the most effective ways to combat the impacts of trauma and maintain a core sense of resilience requires strong, supportive relationships.

Community in Building Resilience

It is a foundational practice for a university supervisor or early career teacher mentor to help the novice educators build resilience and agency with each other and with the supervisor. There must be engagement in the relationship from both sides but there is also power in the interaction. Identifying ways that the relationships can be developed through community together is one strategy to remove the isolating barriers of the teaching profession and explore the best practices that can bolster the self-care of each individual educator. Working together as a community of practice, strategies used regularly in the professional learning community for educators can provide direction and guidance on ways to interact and to leverage the power of numbers.

While it is known that the teaching profession can be isolating (Lortie, 1975), coming together to identify common concerns in a particular district, school, or other educational setting can open doors to possible solutions that may not seem achievable at the individual teacher level. Certainly for those who are early in their career and working to make it through each day, grading period, and year, it can be daunting to imagine advocating for much beyond daily survival. For this group of teachers, a "safety in numbers" approach can make action seem possible and to reassure that the issues being experienced are not usually unique.

What is the collective power of working together to build resilience and, as a result, agency to act? How does this work in pairs, with small groups, etc.? How do mentors or supervisors support each other in this work and work to support novice educators and teacher candidates? This list of questions sparks thoughts about the power of numbers, the importance of relationships in creating caring, protective spaces for teachers to address and react to the realities of the experiences they may have with students who have lived through traumatic events. Resilience is a powerful part of agency relationships with teachers and their mentors.

Agency as a Means for Building Resilience 109

There are practical solutions to these questions addressed in Chapter 7, which will explore the creative ways to build resilience and agency in supervisors.

Perseverance

One of the significant challenges in teacher resilience and agency is the concept of perseverance. How do educators maintain high expectations, skills, and a commitment over time, particularly in the face of children who have experienced intensive, painful, traumatic experiences? More generally defined, one of the challenges of the teaching profession is burnout, regardless of the impact of trauma on the setting or individuals involved. Resilience and agency are crucial for all teachers, whether or not they feel their professional lives to be impacted through experiences with children who have experienced trauma. The work of teaching requires extensive investment. There can be a toll on the educator when the workplace no longer meets the needs of the individual, lacks the necessary supports for professional growth, and/or becomes increasingly complex or fraught with negativity, etc. This can happen without any significant trauma present in the workplace or the lives of the teacher or students, but it certainly occurs with undesired frequency in the teaching profession. Currently, teacher turnover costs districts a significant amount of money each year and results in a great deal of churn for schools, students, and communities as they continually work to build school culture and climate. Creating a stable place for students and teachers is particularly crucial for schools serving communities of color. "Those teaching in schools with 25% or more students of color were more likely to move or leave teaching than teachers in schools with fewer students of color" (Carver-Thomas & Darling-Hammond, 2017). Building resilience in educators, and a sense of agency, is one crucial step toward stemming the tide of teachers leaving the profession while also building the resilience to stay in classrooms working with children facing difficult life experiences.

Teachers and supervisors must work together to find ways to effect change through the sense of agency. This can be built through connections with people who have power or access to it through leadership roles. While the power dynamic may create inequitable situations that make it difficult to affect changes in some cases, it is incumbent on the mentor to continue to model how to reach out and find spaces for conversation, to find strategies for showing best practice in action, and to demonstrate resilience at play—all moves that encourage and reinforce agency, even in the smallest places and means. How do teachers and supervisors find the relationships and spaces to interact with those in power in the school? In the district? How can these relationships be used to effect change in ways that make a difference for educators all the way down to the granular level of daily life in the classroom? Supervisors and new teacher mentors

110   *Agency as a Means for Building Resilience*

have differing levels of access to leaders in the school or district, with new teacher mentors often having more access given their likely status as someone employed by the same district. Regardless, learning to use relationships that exist and working to develop those that do not to ensure that novice educator's needs are met are a crucial expectation of the mentoring role. The collaborating teacher, the grade-level colleagues, the building administrator, plus any others who are important in the life of the early career teacher (or teacher candidate) should be invited to participate in discussion, action, and reflective moments that provide support to the novice. And while invitations to participate in this work may not always be accepted, they should continue to be offered as a sign of openness and willingness to engage in collaborative work to build resilience.

Conclusion

This chapter has tackled the impact of supervisor and teacher agency through the lens of resilience in response to exposure to trauma, which is garnering increasing attention in the educational workplace. As we begin to understand the impact of trauma and toxic stress on the life and development of children, the need for schools and teachers to respond with intentionality and clear strategies for support increases. Teacher preparation must become intimately involved in working to prepare teachers to meet the needs of students who have experienced trauma while also teaching the novice educators how to recognize and address the symptoms of secondary exposure to trauma in themselves. Early career mentoring and supervision also play a role in helping novices to understand and name the experiences they have in the field to better advocate for themselves. This is a powerful and important issue that requires teacher agency to better meet the needs of all involved in these educational relationships. A crucial step toward keeping more teachers in the classroom and avoiding the continuing trend of increasing teacher burnout is using supervisors' agency to act for change for all educators and to model how best to develop resilience and agency in their own right.

References

Abraham-Cook, S. (2012). *The prevalence and correlates of compassion fatigue, compassion satisfaction, and burnout among teachers working in high-poverty urban public schools* (Unpublished doctoral dissertation). Seton Hall University, South Orange, NJ.

Alvarez, H. K. (2007). The impact of teacher preparation on responses to student aggression in the classroom. *Teaching and Teacher Education, 23*, 1113–1126.

Bober, T., Regehr, C., & Zhou, Y. R. (2006). Development of the coping strategies inventory for trauma counselors. *Journal of Loss and Trauma, 11*(1), 71–83.

Burke Harris, N. (2018). *The deepest well: Healing the long-term effects of childhood adversity*. Boston, MA: Houghton Mifflin Harcourt.

Agency as a Means for Building Resilience 111

Carver-Thomas, D., & Darling-Hammond, L. (2017). *Teacher turnover: Why it matters and what we can do about it*. Palo Alto, CA: Learning Policy Institute.

Center for Disease Control and Prevention. (2018). *About adverse childhood experiences*. Retrieved from www.cdc.gov/violenceprevention/acestudy/about_ace.html

Center on the Developing Child, Harvard University. (2018). *Resilience*. Retrieved from https://developingchild.harvard.edu/science/key-concepts/resilience/

Center on the Developing Child. (2015a). *The science of resilience* (In Brief). Retrieved from www.developingchild.harvard.edu

Center on the Developing Child at Harvard University. (2015b). *Supportive relationships and a ctive skill-building strengthen the foundations of resilience: Working paper No. 13*. Retrieved from www.developingchild.harvard.edu

Felitti, V. J., Anda, R. F., Nordenberg, D., Williamson, D. F., Spitz, A. M., Edwards, V., . . . Marks, J. S. (1998). Relationship of childhood abuse and household dysfunction to many of the leading causes of death in adults: The adverse childhood experiences (ACE) study. *American Journal of Preventive Medicine, 14*(4), 245–258.

Figley, C. R. (2002). *Treating compassion fatigue*. New York, NY: Brunner-Routledge.

Hamilton, M. (2008). Compassion fatigue: What school counsellors should know about secondary traumatic stress. *Alberta Counsellor, 30*(1), 9–21.

Hoglund, W. L. G., Klingle, K. E., & Hosan, N. E. (2015). Classroom risks and resources: Teacher burnout, classroom quality and children's adjustment in high needs elementary schools. *Journal of School Psychology, 53*, 337–357.

Hosan, N. E., Hoglund, W. L. G., & Richards, S. (2013, April). *Targeting the classroom quality and children's mental health to promote children's healthy peer relationships*. Paper presented at the 2013 Society for Research in Child Development (SRCD) Biennial Meeting, Seattle, WA.

Kahn, J. H., Schneider, K. T., Jenkins-Henkelman, T. M., & Moyle, L. L. (2006). Emotional social support and job burnout among high-school teachers: Is it all due to dispositional affectivity? *Journal of Organizational Behavior, 27*(6), 793–807.

Lortie, D. (1975). *Schoolteacher: A sociological study*. New York, NY: Simon & Schuster.

Lucas, L. (2007/2008). The pain of attachment—"You have to put a little wedge in there": How vicarious trauma affects child/teacher attachment. *Childhood Education, 84*(2), 85–91.

Monroe, J. F. (1995). Ethical issues associate with secondary trauma in therapists. In B. H. Stamm (Ed.), *Secondary traumatic stress: Self-care issues for clinicians, researchers, and educators* (2nd ed., pp. 211–229). Baltimore, MD: Sidran.

National Center for Mental Health Promotion and Youth Violence Prevention. (2012, July). *Childhood trauma and its effect on healthy development*. Retrieved from http://justice.aksummit.com/PDF/081712_childhood_trauma.pdf

O'Donnell, D. A., Schwab-Stone, M. E., & Muyeed, A. Z. (2002). Multidimensional resilience in urban children exposed to community violence. *Child Development, 73*, 1265–1282.

Pas, E., Bradshaw, C. P., & Hershfeldt, P. A. (2012). Teacher- and school-level predictors of teacher efficacy and burnout: Identifying potential areas of support. *Journal of School Psychology, 50*(1), 129–145.

112 Agency as a Means for Building Resilience

Rice, K., & Groves, B. (2005). *Hope and healing: A caregiver's guide to helping young children affected by trauma.* Washington, DC: Zero to Three.

Souers, K., & Hall, P. (2016). *Fostering resilient learners: Strategies for creating a trauma- sensitive classroom.* Alexandria, VA: Association for Supervision and Curriculum Development.

Stamm, B. H. (2002). Measuring compassion satisfaction as well as fatigue: Developmental history of the compassion satisfaction and fatigue test. In C. R. Figley (Ed.), *Treating compassion fatigue* (pp. 107–119). New York, NY: Brunner-Routledge.

Tonder, C. L., & Williams, C. (2009). Exploring the origins of burnout among secondary educators. *Journal of Industrial Psychology, 55*(1), 1–15.

VanBergeijk, E., & Sarmiento, T. (2006). The consequences of reporting child maltreatment: Are school personnel at risk for secondary traumatic stress? *Brief Treatment and Crisis Intervention, 6*(1), 79–98.

7 Supervision and Mentoring
Applications for Teacher Educators and Administrators

Throughout this text we have provided foundational information on the factors that inform mentors' work, including the history of teacher preparation, goals for encouraging agency among supervisors, and the role of current assessment practices that impact how teachers are supported and evaluated. Together, the environments that today's educators reside in are complex and multilayered. These conditions impact teachers in schools as well as the mentors guiding their work.

This chapter provides a practical overview for teacher educators and those working with supervisors in schools and districts. Content includes recommendations for hands-on professional development activities and learning experiences designed to strengthen the skills and critical thinking of supervisors (i.e., the activity). Specific areas in which supervisors might engage include examinations of personal educational background and their impact on approaches to supervision, the role of school histories on teacher learning and growth, and practical elements of supervision when working with preservice and beginning teachers.

In addition to prompting reflection among supervisors, this chapter presents activities in which supervisors might engage. These include reflections on supervisors' goals, self-studies as a part of action research with beginning teaching, and examinations of school histories and contexts. Also included are explorations of the embeddedness of teacher mentoring as part of national, state, and local requirements for teacher preparation and professional development; considerations of research on supervision as a professional area of study; and finally, specific recommendations for strengthening the technical skills supervisors must exhibit when working with novices. These activities will inform how mentors build professional agency within their own work and with those they support.

Throughout this text we have discussed elements of agency that support supervisors. A focal area is the role of agency as a means of deepening teachers' understanding of one's own practice. Through supervisory support, teachers' work may be strengthened through ongoing reflection and continual learning. To address these aspects of agency, it is necessary

114   *Supervision and Mentoring*

to consider the supports needed to build this capacity in both new and continuing teacher mentors.

In our collective experiences as educators over the past 40 years, we have taught a series of courses designed to address the following areas of supervisory work with beginning teachers:

1. Challenging thinking regarding teachers' work with specific attention to the goals of contemporary P–12 education.
2. Engaging in critical examinations of how teacher mentors enact their work within the context of a teacher preparation program.
3. Teaching the skills for effective supervision and mentoring.
4. Understanding the context of contemporary teacher evaluation systems and their impact on mentoring and supervision.

The outcomes of conversation and reflection across each of these areas provides mentors with a foundational understanding of their roles in teacher education, both within the context of daily work in schools as well as within the mentoring profession. This knowledge base fortifies professional agency by equipping educators with a big picture understanding of teacher education across the career continuum and the impact on work as mentors.

Supervisors and Mentors: Stakeholders in Teacher Preparation

As part of the candidate experiences offered in our teacher preparation programs, preservice teachers reflect on their viewpoints regarding the education profession and their emerging roles as classroom educators. We push our preservice teachers to consider how their beliefs and values inform their professional identities and how they are manifest in their daily work. Across multiple courses and various assignments, we encourage consideration on what it means to teach P–12 students and help teacher candidates come to understand that teachers' work is complex and multidimensional. For teacher educators, similar investigations are valuable. On one level, explorations of one's stance as a supervisor reveals personal beliefs about education and places those beliefs within the broader context of teacher education and professional development. Beyond general awareness, these explorations by supervisors also have the potential to increase their personal agency and the agency of the teachers with whom they work. Specifically, the mentors' understanding of how their role is situated within the broader educational context allows them to impact change.

In their positions, supervisors have the capacity to enhance the leadership potential and empowerment of their mentees through professional development and reflection. In turn, supervisors experience similar ownership as leaders and active participants in systems change. Supervisors experience similar levels of agency through the knowledge gained by impacting teachers' work. Supervisors understand their own backgrounds, recognize the impact of contexts, and practice leadership as members of communities who advance the practice of teaching (Rust & Freidus, 2001). Their knowledge as teacher leaders informs their mentoring work and enhances their roles as active participants in teacher education.

Individual Histories

Preservice teachers consider how their experiences as P–12 students have impacted their approaches to teaching and their general views on education in the context of teacher preparation courses and clinical placements. These reflections are useful in that they prompt consideration of the ways in which the values, goals, and practices within schools and classrooms shape identities and expectations for teachers' work.

For educators at all levels, research on an individual's P–12 school experiences underscores the influence of individual journeys and histories on daily work in classrooms and schools (Calderhead, 1991; Bullough & Gitlin, 2001; Holt-Reynolds, 1992; Knowles, 1992, 1993). The relationship between an individual's history and their current practices are particularly critical in that educational backgrounds inform views on the purposes of school, learners, instruction, curriculum, and assessment. The influence of one's background and experience are significant for teacher educators and those working as mentors. While an acknowledgment of our personal history is a first step, educators must also engage in reflections and critical analyses of how educational pasts positively or negatively impact teaching and mentoring.

At the preservice level, repositories of the artifacts from course or field experiences are gathered within professional portfolios. Course readings and related assignments may include personal history papers, autobiographies, or the compilation of "artifacts" designed to capture individual stories. Preservice teachers are provided with the opportunity to reflect on their storytelling, over time. For example, by revisiting assignments within the context of courses that address their experiences with curriculum, pedagogy, assessment, or classroom management, preservice teachers begin to see the thematic tethers that build a tapestry of how backgrounds inform expectations, standards, and goal setting for their students.

Teacher mentors might also engage in similar efforts to reflect on their histories and backgrounds within a course or a professional development experience. For example, as adult learners, mentors are also in the position to advance professionally. Taking ownership in their own professional development might include documenting and showcasing professional

116 *Supervision and Mentoring*

improvement through guided reflection and active engagement with others with specific examinations of how one's educational past has impacted approaches to mentoring. This acknowledges the ways in which supervisors' backgrounds and histories impact their work (Bates, Drits, & Ramirez, 2011). These components of professional development for mentors expand the traditions of past supervisory support that were often didactic and problem-solving in nature. A reciprocal process of learning between mentors and beginning teachers fosters a process that acknowledges and validates work with others (Rust & Freidus, 2001).

Reflections on personal histories result in mentors that are better poised to pose questions and prompt thought among beginning teachers that encourage in-depth explorations of teaching practices. Analyses of the conditions of schools, and an increased awareness of the relationships between teachers and students, informs expectations for what takes place within the context of daily teaching (Dantas-Whitney, 2016; Griffin, Watson, & Liggett, 2016; Ronfeldt, 2015). Without the perspective taking that emerges when all levels of educators examine their backgrounds and related experiences, approaches to curriculum, pedagogy, and assessment may remain static and somewhat insular.

Supervisors and Their Work

As a natural extension of reflections on one's past, we also ask supervisors to examine *their* existing beliefs regarding their work with beginning teachers. Areas for consideration include reflections by mentors regarding their views of supervision as a component of teacher preparation and acknowledging the distinct role of supervisors within the context of student teaching and practicum experiences.

Recent pronouncements from the American Association of Colleges of Teacher Education (AACTE, 2018) reference the need for greater clarity and agreement in the roles we assign for those working as teacher educators, and as school-based educators. The deliberate naming and delineation of roles among these stakeholders provides definition to the work of participants in the student teaching or professional development enterprise. Chapter 2 of this book highlights both historical assignments of these individuals as well as more current roles assumed as mentors contribute more to the teaching equation that just evaluation.

In addition to understanding the specific components of supervisory and mentoring roles as discussed in Chapter 2, the purpose of student teaching or practicum must also be delineated and understood. Student teaching and/or practicum experiences may serve many purposes. An obvious purpose is to provide preservice teachers practical experience under the guide of a mentor. Here, pedagogical skill development and opportunities to learn more about daily life in classrooms is the focus.

Additionally, classroom-based experiences serve as opportunities for novice educators to reflect deeply on the interplay between multiple variables such as instructional delivery, curriculum choices, and assessment and how they are evident in daily teaching. As key players, the position of the mentors is vital to push teachers' thinking in ways that are deep and distinctive (e.g., the impact of race, culture and gender on interactions between teachers and students, the role of assessment, curricular decisions). However, to engage in this work, mentors must understand their own perspectives and experiences. In doing so, they are able to lead others in ways that acknowledge their own histories and backgrounds to better inform and impact their leadership with others.

Under the direction of faculty members in a teacher education program or those working with practicing teachers at the school or district level, periodic examinations of perspectives regarding supervision take place over time. To encourage reflection among supervisors, exchanges may take place using face-to-face methods or online discussions. The goal of engaging in professional dialogue is to prompt reflection on beliefs about the role of supervision and mentoring. Providing opportunities for mentors to debrief these dialogues with a more experienced supervisor or teacher educator facilitates greater self-awareness through engagement in these self-analyses. These explorations allow supervisors to become cognizant of their supervisory practices and how their histories inform the ways in which they engage with their mentees. For example, in order to understand the vantage points and the merits of perspective taking, mentors will be asked to share their views and intentions in their work as mentors and to explore how their beliefs impact practices. Educational issues designed to inform conversations in professional communities that promote supervisors' critical thinking include:

1. Understanding perspectives on the purpose of school.
2. Examining views of learners in today's classrooms and schools.
3. Exploring beliefs regarding learner diversity and its role in their work.
4. Identifying fundamental goals of educators, as a group, and delineating the actions they will take to meet these goals within the context of daily teaching.

These prompts offer guides for thinking about a number of important issues related to educators' daily work for supervisors as well as the beginning teachers with whom they work.

While the reflection that is generated through these questions is obviously important, educators must also examine whether there are disconnects between what they believe and what actually happens as they work in communities of practice. The dialogue in these professional conversations serves as a safe place to practice the art of challenging oneself and

118 *Supervision and Mentoring*

others to describe, defend, and clarify ideas with the intent to learn and grow from the experience.

As described in the text introduction, making one's stance explicit fosters the development of agency when individuals consider their beliefs and envision how viewpoints will be articulated and understood by others. Sharing views "publicly" requires reflection and opportunities that underscore the unique contribution of each supervisor in their work. Being able to articulate and expound on these stances is crucial, as it forces consideration about how these articulated stances will be enacted in practice with mentees. Considering what it might look like to embed these stances in practice, and receiving feedback on those ideas, is necessary to make the bridge from theory to enactment.

Perspectives from Professional Communities

Now more than ever, those working in classrooms and schools must consider a range of factors when planning for teaching and evaluating practice. As discussed throughout this text, explorations of beliefs about children and families, and the associated responsibilities of their professional roles, inform educators' beliefs about teachers' work. These personal reflections are important, though limited. Without more guided prompts between educators, reflections may take place in isolation. At the core of these efforts is the underlying goal of encouraging critical reflection among communities of educators as a vehicle for informing decision-making. However, without dedicated prompts and posing questions that challenge thinking, discussions may result in rather vacuous recaps of daily happenings. Alfie Kohn (2006) pushes educators to think about how their practices align with the espoused goals and values.

In his seminal work on community building within classrooms and schools, author and researcher Alfie Kohn (2006) encourages educators to consider their beliefs and the manifestation of those beliefs within their daily work. He argues for examinations of the ways in which underlying intentions may impact teaching, unintentionally. Kohn suggests that while many educators claim to espouse certain values and beliefs, their choices and actions may run counter as they work in classrooms. While laudable goals often embody generalized priorities for teaching and learning, Kohn (2006) argues that there may be a disconnectedness between broad-based goals and the actions in which educators engage on a daily basis.

Central to Kohn's argument is the need for educators to examine their practices to determine if their teaching or interactions are distancing them from their students and subsequently diminishing the potential for community building. One way of situating Kohn's proposal is for mentors to frame their questions and guidance with preservice and in-service teachers through examples that highlight how actions may play out in the classroom in ways that are unintended. For example, educators may espouse independent decision-making and critical thinking, yet their assignments, pedagogy, classroom management, and assessment strategies may not support these goals. The ensuing dialogue between educators creates an environment where they consider how they will create learning spaces that foster the community as envisioned. This is no simple task, and is not an exercise exclusively geared toward teachers in P–12 classrooms. The same process may take place for teacher educators. This dilemma places mentors in a particularly critical role.

Educational Contexts

School and classroom histories have an impact on the daily work of educators (Bullough & Gitlin, 2001). Through investigations into school histories educators are provided with data-gathering activities designed to push their thinking beyond the surface toward historical practices and conventions that influence daily happenings. For example, an often overlooked area of study is the role of the traditions and cultures within classrooms (Barth, 2002). Practices might include ways where some students are acknowledged or honored over others—the role of athletics in a school community or viewpoints on family engagement. These histories are part of the fabric of schools that inform practices such as perspectives on ability, leadership, diversity, curriculum decisions, assessment, pedagogies, and family community involvement. By making these sometimes more subtle components of schools more visible, educators' agency is enhanced in ways that inform decision-making. A general awareness of contexts and the history of a school or district provides mentors with background information as means of guiding mentoring and supervision. Understanding a school culture, the community outside of the school, and leadership within a district provides a unique profile of the idiosyncrasies of the settings where teachers reside by informing how those histories and traditions impact curriculum choices, school culture, and daily operations.

Supervisors might consider the following areas on how best to support the teachers with whom they are working:

1. What are the demographics of the community where my student teacher(s) are placed?
2. What are the priorities and initiatives of the district where my student teacher(s) are working? For example, if technology integration is a goal for the district, how might that play out in the type of evaluation and observational support provided to teachers?
3. How do factors such as community goals and engagement impact the mission and agenda of the school and classrooms? How do stakeholder groups inform teachers' work? Knowing about the roles and

120 *Supervision and Mentoring*

responsibilities of parent–teacher associations, school boards, community councils, etc. sheds light on the community where educators reside.

While the work of mentors certainly follows a predictable flow in terms of observations, providing feedback, and encouraging reflection and dialogue among communities of educators, this work does not exist in isolation. Data regarding classrooms, schools, and districts are embedded into the daily work of educators and drive a number of decisions. Understanding the nuances of education communities provides the context necessary for decision-making, reflection, and the enhancement of agency through informed understandings of the factors that impact school cultures.

Research and Educational Practitioners

Educators' professional work is informed by both research and practical applications to classrooms and schools (Zeichner, 2018). Research on teacher preparation addresses many dimensions of teachers' work in ways that are theoretical, empirical, and applied. Research emphases includes examinations of social foundations in education, teaching and learning, learner diversity, technology, curriculum and assessment, and professional development.

In addition to research on the technical elements of teachers' work (i.e., skill development and measurement), educational research also encompasses more broad-based areas related to teacher education and teacher professional development (i.e., educator growth and advancement over time). Researchers and practitioners examine areas such as how teacher reflection and teaching adaptations build professional agency. By becoming intellectually engaged in teacher education research, mentors are exposed to a range of perspectives and viewpoints related to teaching and learning and how those areas will apply to their own roles as supervisors.

Mentors, as teacher educators, are encouraged to engage with other professionals at the state or local level through explorations of educational research and its applications to classrooms. For example, exposure and participation with colleagues at the local level provides professional platforms to examine both traditional and more practice-based research on teaching and learning. Collaboration with supervision peers from the same institution or district can provide opportunities to engage in debriefing research, share best practices from applied research, or work together to identify questions for further research. Additionally, affiliations with professional organizations offer a professional network among supervisors as members of the teacher education community.

Professional organizations offer educators a community committed to the advancement of the profession. The premier research organization for teacher education is the American Educational Research Association

Supervision and Mentoring 121

(AERA). Self-described as "a national research society, [that] strives to advance knowledge about education, to encourage scholarly inquiry related to education, and to promote the use of research to improve education and serve the public good" (AERA, 2018), AERA provides researchers and practitioners with scholarly inquiry and the dissemination of that work.

Another advocacy and research organization is the American Association of Colleges of Teacher Education (AACTE), a group committed to informing educator preparation, sharing research on teacher education, and guiding policy in areas including, but not limited to, supervision, mentoring, and teacher evaluation. Many states have local chapters of AACTE for collaboration among statewide professionals in educator preparation that serve as an additional opportunity for collegial interaction and collaboration. Additionally, Phi Delta Kappa (PDK) and the Association for Supervision and Curriculum Development (ASCD) are additional organizations committed to the education community. Affiliations with professional organizations committed to the work of teacher professional development and teacher preparation offer a recognition of the collective power of stakeholders.

The following activities and assignments offer teacher educators practical experiences to encourage their mentors to participate. The focal areas provide prompts for reflection in ways designed to encourage informed decision making as mentors provide guidance for others. These activities create opportunities where mentors expand their knowledge of systems as active participants in teacher preparation.

Action Research and Self-Study

Action research is a framework that allows educators to consider a systematic process of self-reflection that capitalizes on data-based decision-making (Bullough & Gitlin, 2001; Carr & Kemmis, 1986: Johnson, 2009, 2014; Somekh & Zeichner, 2009). For this activity, supervisors are asked to prepare a research proposal in an area of interest within the field of teacher preparation linked to classroom-based mentoring. Both informal and more formal structures may be implemented as educators consider how they will gather data on practice and how they will disseminate their findings. Central to an action research format for those working as mentors are components of systematic investigations related to the explicit work of supervisors. Self-studies are a particular type of investigation that will provide supervisors with critical self-analyses. Topics mentors might consider as part of an action research project include, but are not limited to:

1. Effectiveness of mentoring strategies using survey and interview data.
2. Examinations of electronic feedback as a tool for identifying teaching episodes for analysis and review.

122 *Supervision and Mentoring*

3. Analyses of language when providing feedback to preservice and in-service teachers.
4. Identifying effective strategies for building community among preservice and in-service teachers as part of the mentoring and supervisory process.

In order to operationalize plans for systematic self-reflection, those in supervisory positions might consider both formal and informal outlets for their writing. Informal activities might take the place of data gathering and analyses as part of professional learning communities (see Chapter 5) or site-based school improvement efforts. A key to how these activities take place is within the context of educators working as colleagues versus in isolation. The group dynamic of this work builds a collegial tenor and also allows for multiple perspectives on decision-making (Cochran-Smith & Lytle, 1993).

Supervisors might consider asking, "What are others doing within the field of education in areas related to effective mentoring?" This exploratory process, while likely only in a format for discussion, provides those who are studying supervision a framework for completing a task analysis for a specific area of study in the future.

The assignment may allow supervisors to actually engage in a research project or self-study or simply provide an opportunity for questions regarding their work for problem-solving. Formal project components likely include standard points for consideration such as the following:

1. Research objective
2. Proposed research question(s)
3. Proposed methods, techniques, or modes of inquiry
4. Proposed data sources, evidence, objects, or materials

While self-studies and action research provide educators with tangible outcomes regarding their practices as teachers and mentors, it would be remiss to discount the impact of policies that inform the work of P–12 and teacher educators. The following provides an introduction into the oversight that guides, and sometimes constricts, educators' work.

Dimensions of Teacher Preparation Programs

A fine-grained analysis of the policies and procedures that govern teacher preparation provides insights into factors that inform programmatic decision-making for those working as supervisors. The following activities encourage reflection on the operational frameworks within teacher preparation. By understanding the workings of the oversight bodies for teacher education, accreditation bodies for example, supervisors are provided with perspective on decision-making for teacher mentoring.

National and State Accreditation: Implications for Supervisors and Mentors

Teacher preparation programs across the United States are required to adhere to the standards established by local and national organizations. Organizations such as the Council for the Accreditation of Educator Preparation (CAEP) as well as state licensure and evaluation bodies identify the criteria and indicators of performance that are used to determine program quality. As such, teacher preparation programs within colleges and universities are required to adhere to the standards for program approval affiliated with these oversight bodies. Depending upon the compliance responsibilities of a particular institution, documentation varies, but typically includes capturing the details of program operations and efforts to ensure quality teacher preparation from various stakeholders.

To broaden the insights of supervisors, teacher educators and school or district administrators are encouraged to learn about and share their respective institutions' accreditation or program approval requirements. The standards, data collection, and review process provide unique insights and clarification for those working in supervisory positions. Knowing the workings of an agency is both informative and empowering for any member of an education community.

Because there are specific criteria related to supervisory training, support, and data collection, a review of policies and procedures is informative and can guide specific expectations for how teachers' work is to be evaluated. Policy reviews might include an analysis of requirements for observations of teaching, discussions of how partnerships are embedded within P–12 settings, data collection efforts, or a discussion of how program requirements impact supervision and mentoring in the preparation of teachers. Following a policy review, supervisors are invited to consider recommendations for enhancing teacher and supervisory agency through discussions and recommendations for improving existing policies. This opportunity for ownership over one's profession gives educators the opportunity to contribute to or at least consider their contributions in teacher preparation and professional feedback sharing.

Evaluating Supervisory Feedback

In order to evaluate supervisors' competencies, this activity is designed to record and assess supervisory episodes where supervisors are providing feedback to their mentees. Specifically, mentors capture video or audio recordings of feedback session(s) with a preservice or in-service teacher. Obviously, the necessary permission process must take place to ensure anonymity and identity protection as part of the filming or taping process. Key areas for a post-video review address the ways in which the mentor offers support, feedback, or general interactions. Specific focal

124 *Supervision and Mentoring*

areas within the context of the video analysis may include, but are not limited to:

1. Effective communication (e.g., appropriate eye contact; active listening).
2. Specificity of feedback, versus broad generalizations, that may be difficult to define or identify.
3. References within the feedback shared during supervisory sessions that include linkages to evaluation or program criteria.
4. The use of reflective prompts that require teachers to consider broad-based issues, in addition to skill development.

Knowledge of broad-based issues that inform supervision are important components in these educators' work (e.g., policies and procedures, reflection; educational research; tools for professional learning communities). In addition, supervisors and mentors must also possess explicit technical skills that support the development and reflective practices for preservice and beginning teachers. These skills are particularly critical during feedback sessions where prompts for reflection are tethered to actions that reflect the knowledge of both research on best practice and the ability to translate those dimensions into daily teaching.

Practically, supervisors must consider the technical elements of providing feedback. The following recommendations from Henry and Weber (2016) offer insight for mentors as they consider the readiness and receptivity of their mentees to grow in ways that support both skill development as well as prompts that challenge whether they are truly meant for the profession. Questions for consideration by supervisors:

1. Does the preservice teacher possess the aptitude for teaching? Do they understand teachers' work? Do they recognize and value the students in their care?
2. To what extent is the timing right for each individual as they consider the completion of a professional preparation program? That is, do they have the time, resources, and support network to engage in the work of a licensure or professional training experience?
3. To what extent is the candidate open to and able to learn the skills necessary for effective teaching (e.g., instruction, classroom management, curriculum development, assessment)?
4. Is the teacher with whom the supervisor is working self-reflective and able to evaluate and judge their strengths and areas in need of development?

In answering these questions, supervisors must be able to facilitate experiences, conduct evaluations, and offer guidance that leads their mentees toward resolution to these specific areas of focus. The aforementioned questions serve as prompts for supervisor in their work and in their own reflections of their mentees' growth.

Performance Assessments and Portfolio Development

Increasingly, a performance assessment is required of educators as a means of demonstrating teaching competencies (Reagan, Schram, McCurdy, Chang, & Evans, 2016; Stewart, Scalzo, Merino, & Nilsen, 2015). Among the tools used to showcase these skills are teaching portfolios. Chapter 4 of this book provides additional information on ways which portfolio development may be used as a criterion toward National Board Certification, for example. Portfolio creation may provide a vehicle for documenting supervisors' work in ways that are tangible and highlight the accomplishments of those involved in professional advancement.

Similar to the documents developed by teachers, supervisors are invited to develop a supervision portfolio that showcases a purposeful collection of their work. For supervisors, performance assessments allow mentors a space to showcase concrete examples of leadership, reflective practice, and understanding of research on professional practice. Over time, the representations of work may include activities in which mentors engage with their mentees, field notes, personal observations, and other artifacts that allow supervisors to document what they are learning in their roles within the context of their work, including demonstrations of growth in their thinking. Further, the reflective process that is central to quality portfolio development enhances professional ownership and agency. To that end, those preparing supervisors might encourage the development of a professional portfolio as a venue to exhibit and document efforts, progress, and achievements in one or more areas of supervision.

Conclusion

As teacher educators, supervisors are tasked with complex and layered work. They are in the position to nurture experiences for beginning teachers that allow them to advance in their work and to prosper, over time. Research and practice in teacher preparation and professional development often address ways to foster these goals for both preservice and in-service teachers, but rarely do we consider the "self-work" necessary for supervisors to advance in their personal agency. This chapter has offered insights that provide these critical stakeholders with experiences for their agency development in ways that are explicit and applied. The futures of supervisors are equally critical in the education enterprise.

References

American Association of Colleges of Teacher Education. (2018). *A pivot toward clinical practice, its lexicon, and the renewal of educator preparation.* Washington, DC: Author.

American Educational Research Association (AERA). (2018). Retrieved from www.aera.net/

Barth, R. (2002). The culture. *Educational Leadership, 9,* 6–11.

126 Supervision and Mentoring

Bates, A. J., Drits, D., & Ramirez, L. (2011). Self-awareness and enactment of supervisory stance: Influences on responsiveness toward student teacher learning. *Teacher Education Quarterly*, 38(3), 69–87.

Bullough, R. V., & Gitlin, A. (2001). *Becoming a student of teaching: Linking knowledge production and practice of teaching* (2nd ed.). New York, NY: Routledge.

Calderhead, J. (1991). The nature and growth of knowledge in student teaching. *Teaching and Teacher Education*, 7(5/6), 531–535.

Carr, W., & Kemmis, S. (1986). *Becoming critical: Education, knowledge and action research*. London: Falmer Press.

Cochran-Smith, M., & Lytle, S. L. (1993). *Inside/outside: Teacher research and knowledge*. New York, NY: Teachers College Press.

Dantas-Whitney, M. (2016). Problematizing assumptions, examining dilemmas, and exploring promising possibilities in culturally relevant pedagogy. A response to "I didn't see it as a cultural thing": Supervisors of student teachers define and describe culturally responsive supervision. *Democracy & Education*, 24(1), 1–4. Retrieved from http://democracyeducationjournal.org/home/

Griffin, L. B., Watson, D., & Liggett, T. (2016). "I didn't see it as a cultural thing": Supervisors of student teachers define and describe culturally responsive supervision. *Democracy & Education*, 24(1), 1–13. Retrieved from http://democracyeducationjournal.org/

Henry, M., & Weber, A. (2016). *Evaluating a student teacher*. New York, NY: Rowman & Littlefield Education.

Holt-Reynolds, D. (1992). Personal history-based beliefs as relevant prior knowledge in course work. *American Educational Research Journal*, 29(2), 325–349.

Johnson, A. (2014). *A short guide to action research* (4th ed.). New York, NY: Pearson.

Johnson, A. (2009). *What every teacher should know about action research*. Upper Saddle River, NJ: Pearson.

Knowles, J. G. (1992). Models for understanding pre-service and beginning teachers' biography. In I. F. Goodson (Ed.), *Studying teachers' lives*. London: Routledge.

Knowles, J. G. (1993). Life history accounts as mirrors: A practical avenue for the conceptualization of reflection in teacher education. In J. Calderhead & P. Gates (Eds.), *Conceptualizing reflection in teacher development*. London: Falmer Press.

Kohn, A. (2006). *Beyond discipline: From compliance to community*. Alexandria, VA: Association for Supervision and Curriculum Development.

Reagan, E. M., Schram, T., McCurdy, K., Chang, T-H., & Evans, C. M. (2016). Politics of policy: Assessing the implementation, impact, and evolution of the Performance Assessment for California Teachers (PACT) and edTPA. *Education Policy Analysis Archives*, 24(9), 1–27. http://dx.doi.org/10.14507/epaa.v24.2176

Ronfeldt, M. (2015). Field placement schools and instructional effectiveness. *Journal of Teacher Education*, 66(4), 304–320. doi:10.1177/0022487115592463

Rust, F. O., & Freidus, H. (Eds.). (2001). *Guiding school change: The role of work of change agents*. New York, NY: Teachers College Press.

Somekh, B., & Zeichner, K. (2009). Action research for educational reform: Remodeling action research theories and practices in local contexts. *Educational Action Research*, 17(1), 5–21.

Stewart, A., Scalzo, J., Merino, N., & Nilsen, K. (2015). Beyond the criteria: Evidence of teacher learning in performance assessment. *Teacher Education Quarterly, 42*(3), 33–58.

Zeichner, K. (2018). *The struggle for the soul of teacher education.* New York, NY: Routledge.

Recommended Readings for Those Working with Supervisors and Mentors

Purposes of Teacher Education and the Climate in the US

Darling-Hammond, L. (2016). Research on teaching and teacher education and its influences on policy and practice. *Educational Researcher, 45*(2), 83–91. doi:10.3102/0013189X16639597

Darling-Hammond, L. (2010). Teacher education and the American future. *Journal of Teacher Education, 61*(1–2), 35–47. doi:10.1177/0022487109348024

Goodwin, A. L., Smith, L., Souto-Manning, M., Cheruvu, R., Tan, M. Y., Reed, R., & Taveras, L. (2014). What should teacher educators know and be able to do? Perspectives from practicing teacher educators. *Journal of Teacher Education, 65*(4), 284–302. doi:10.1177/0022487114535266

Grossman, P., & McDonald, M. (2008). Back to the future: Directions for research in teaching and teacher education. *American Educational Research Journal, 45*(1), 184–205. doi:10.3102/0002831207312906

Why Bother with Reflection?

Clara, M. (2014). What is reflection? Looking for clarity in an ambiguous notion. *Journal of Teacher Education,66*(3),261–271.doi:10.1177/0022487114552028

Hayden, H., & Chiu, M. M. (2015). Reflective teaching via a problem exploration-teaching adaptations-resolution cycle: A mixed methods study of preservice teachers' reflective notes. *Journal of Mixed Methods Research, 9,* 133–151. doi:10.1177/1558689813509027

Kalchman, M. (2015). Focusing on reflective practice: Reconsidering field experiences for urban teacher preparation. *Perspectives on Urban Education, 12*(1), 3–17. Retrieved from www.urbanedjournal.org/

Kim, Y., & Silver, R. E. (2016). Provoking reflective thinking in post observation conversations. *Journal of Teacher Education, 67*(3), 203–219. doi:10.1177/0022487116637120

Zeichner, K. M. (1994). Research on teacher thinking and different view of reflective practice in teaching and teacher education. In I. Carlgren, G. Handal, & S. Vaage (Eds.), *Teachers' minds and research on teachers' thinking and practice* (pp. 9–27). London: Falmer Press.

Culturally Responsive Supervision

Bates, A. J., & Rosaen, C. (2010). Making sense of classroom diversity: How can field instruction practices support interns' learning? *Studying Teacher Education, 6*(1), 45–61. doi:10.1080/17425961003669151

128 *Supervision and Mentoring*

Lincove, J., Osborne, C., Mills, N., & Bellows, L. (2015). Teacher preparation for profit or Prestige: Analysis of a diverse market for teacher preparation. *Journal of Teacher Education*, 66(5), 415–434. doi:10.1177/0022487115602311

The Business of Teacher Quality

Gargani, J., & Strong, M. (2015). Response to "Rating teachers cheaper, faster, and better: Not so fast": It's about evidence. *Journal of Teacher Education*, 66(4), 395–401. doi:10.1177/0022487115587110

Good, T. L., & Lavigne, A. L. (2015). Rating teachers cheaper, faster, and better: Not so fast. *Journal of Teacher Education*, 66(3), 288–293. doi:10.1177/0022487115574292

Grossman, P., Cohen, J., Ronfeldt, M., & Brown, L. (2014). The test matters: The relationship between classroom observation scores and teacher value added on multiple types of assessment. *Educational Researcher*, 43(6), 293–303. doi:10.3102/0013189x14544542

Assessment Tools and Goals

Bates, A. J., & Burbank, M. D. (2008). Effective student teacher supervision in the era of No Child Left Behind. *The Professional Educator*, 32(2), 1–11.

Ledwell, K., & Oyler, C. (2016). Unstandardized responses to a "standardized" test: The edTPA as gatekeeper and curriculum change agent. *Journal of Teacher Education*, 67(2), 120–134. doi:10.1177/0022487115624739

Sato, M. (2014). What is the underlying conception of teaching of the edTPA? *Journal of Teacher Education*, 65(5), 421–434. doi:10.1177/0022487114542518

Triads in Supervision: Whose Knowledge Counts?

Bullough, R. V., & Draper, R. J. (2004). Making sense of a failed triad: Mentors, university supervisors, and positioning theory. *Journal of Teacher Education*, 55(5), 407–420. doi:10.1177/0022487114561659

Clarke, A., Triggs, V., & Nielsen, W. (2014). Cooperating teacher participation in teacher education: A review of the literature. *Review of Educational Research*, 84(2), 163–202. doi:10.3102/0034654313499618

Tillema, H. (2009). Assessment for learning to teach appraisal of practice teaching lessons by mentors, supervisors, and student teachers. *Journal of Teacher Education*, 60(2), 155–167. doi:10.1177/0022487108330551

Wolff, C. E., Van den Bogert, N., Jarodzka, H., & Boshuizen, H. P. (2014). Keeping an eye on learning: Differences between expert and novice teachers' representations of classroom management events. *Journal of Teacher Education*, 66(1), 68–85. doi:10.1177/0022487114549810

The Contexts of Supervision

Burbank, M. D., Bates, A. J., & Gupta, U. (2016). The influence of teacher development on preservice supervision: A case study across content areas. *The Teacher Educator*, 51, 55–69. doi:10.1080/08878730.2015.1107441

Desimone, L. M., Hochberg, E. D., Porter, A. C., Polikoff, M. S., Schwartz, R., & Johnson, L. J. (2013). Formal and informal mentoring: Complementary, compensatory, or consistent? *Journal of Teacher Education*, 65(2), 88–110. doi:10.1177/0022487113511643

Ronfeldt, M. (2015). Field placement schools and instructional effectiveness. *Journal of Teacher Education*, 66(4), 304–320. doi:10.1177/0022487115592463

Valencia, S., Martin, S., Place, N., & Grossman, P. (2009). Complex interaction in student teaching: Lost opportunities for learning. *Journal of Teacher Education*, 60(3), 304–322. doi:10.117/0022487109336543

Zeichner, K. M., & Gore, J. M. (1990). Teacher socialization. In W. R. Houston & J. Sikula (Eds.), *Handbook of research on teacher education* (pp. 329–348). New York, NY: Palgrave Macmillan.

8 Conclusion

Classrooms and schools are dynamic and vibrant communities. Demographic changes across the United States, demands for an educated populace, increased accountability and transparency for P–16 educators, and the ubiquitous integration of technology are commonplace. In response to the world around us, teacher preparation and professional development must engage in ways that provide educators with the support they need to prosper. Supervisors are particularly well poised to address the realities of life in classrooms through the professional guidance they offer other educators as they grow and advance in their careers.

Explicit training and professional development for supervisors encourage agency by empowering them in their work with beginning teachers. However, quality supervisory training does not happen without a strategic plan, follow up, and ongoing support. Like other education professionals, supervisors must be provided with experiences that guide their work as a means of strengthening their craft (Levine, 2011). Without this support, the efforts of supervisors are often isolated and reduced to individual cases of success or failure rather than the impactful collective influence on educational practice that agency can offer.

As described in the introduction and reinforced throughout this text, in order for supervisors to have an impact they must be able to navigate the immediate needs of teachers' work as well as the goals of those across education circles. These dual emphases underscore the balancing act for supervisors as they lead others. Therefore, a first step to enhancing supervisor agency is to acknowledge that this work does not occur in isolation. Educating, empowering, and facilitating supervisors is a collective endeavor. As members of education teams, supervisors work in reciprocity with teachers to guide their growth in the earliest stages of their development. This process serves to empower both supervisors and teachers in ways that allow them to engage in the profession as inquiring, intentional, and thoughtful leaders of students and communities.

This chapter weaves together elements of supervisor agency as a dimension of teacher development. We explore the implications of text themes on supervisors' work in today's classrooms and schools. We offer

Conclusion 131

recommendations for best practices in fostering agency and suggest that the reality of guiding and mentoring teachers is an ongoing process. Within the context of our discussion we pose a number of questions and topics that might be used to continue conversations in supervisory settings around the country.

Developing Teacher Practices

Twenty-first century education requires that key players within school settings recognize the varying perspectives on the purposes of school and related goals for P–12 education. This acknowledgment allows educators to approach their work through informed decision-making. For example, educators who recognize the dynamic nature of teaching and learning understand that schools are a reflection of society on both macro and micro levels, and subsequently act on this perspective for their students. Supervisors with this information are able to foster environments that empower educators in ways that inform practice. This process for supervisors is twofold. The science and art of supervisors' work is to inform teachers' practical skills while simultaneously shaping the direction of professional learning, decision-making, and agency. The role of school contexts, including those supporting clinical practice, and professional communities of practice are particularly critical in these efforts.

Calls to strengthen clinical practice include increasing attention to content, pedagogy, and an acknowledgment of the role of contexts (AACTE, 2013, 2018) on the part of teacher preparation programs. Leaders in the field are also encouraging efforts to increase quality clinical experiences (AACTE, 2013, 2018; Zeichner, 2012, 2017). These foundational responsibilities for attending to the intersecting elements of teaching are among the reasons why supervisory support is critical. This text has addressed both the essential need for supervisors who understand the context of teachers' lives in classrooms as well as the nature of the contexts themselves. This recognition is particularly critical at a time within teacher education when the number of alternative routes to licensure and nuances across district-level professional development experiences are increasing.

Because teacher preparation and professional development vary, mentoring and supervision must include training and related growth plans that strengthen teachers' skills as well as the dispositions necessary for effectively serving all students. In their roles, supervisors are in the position to empower educators through the agency that develops when their work is informed by research on best practices and when professionals build communities of practice who collaboratively tackle tough challenges. This melding allows for professional dialogue that advances thinking and teaching through informed decision-making among cadres of educators. Supervisory leadership supports effective communication and nurtures dialogue as a means of advancing practice.

132 *Conclusion*

Facilitating Supervisor Agency

In order to lead, supervisors must also have agency about their practice. Supervisors with agency have voice, inspiring others to consider the impact of their practices on the lives of students, families, and communities (Bates & Burbank, 2008; Bates, Drits, & Ramirez, 2011; Bates, Ramirez, & Drits, 2009; Bates & Rosaen, 2010; Burbank, Bates, & Gupta, 2016; Burbank, Ramirez, & Bates, 2012; Rust & Freidus, 2001). "Agency connotes dynamic momentum by finding voice, progress by making choice, forward movement by taking ownership, and strength by leading change" (Gallavan & Webster-Smith, 2012, p. 54). This momentum is a powerful tool to guide and promote change within classrooms and schools.

Voice and Empowerment

Supervisor voice, used in advocacy for others, is a form of empowerment that reflects the realized potential of an advanced educator. As education experts, supervisors who are empowered are better able to act on behalf of others. In these situations they teach, model, and motivate. For example, modeling use of voice on issues of access, equity, and best practices for instruction is a particularly powerful means of guiding a novice educator as part of early career development. The process is complex and challenging, particularly within today's classrooms and schools where there are many competing needs and initiatives vying for teachers' time and attention.

One of the most crucial aspects of empowerment is the ability to tackle controversial issues in educational settings with grace but also with an emphasis on making progress or taking action. With the increasing diversity of the student population in the United States, teachers must be empowered with knowledge informed by research and historical practices that have often negatively impacted generations of learners. Supervisors with agency possess the voice, skills, and knowledge to inform others' work in their collective efforts to challenge educational practices that marginalize students from a range of backgrounds. Building positive school cultures that meet the needs of all learners is an ongoing challenge for educators and school leaders. Supervisors who use their voice and empowerment to engage around these issues in support of novice educators are realizing their agency in ways that can make a difference for all learners. To meet these goals, supervisors who engage in varied relationships are able to create a sense of connectedness for professional problem-solving.

Connectedness

Supervisors possess varied relationships in school settings that create a sense of connectedness, providing diverse perspectives on and opportunities for discussion about educational issues and practices. Harnessing

Conclusion 133

the power of these relationships to impact practice, impart insights on current trends and challenges, and collectively navigate changes in education is a skill that supervisors with agency engage with finesse. Novice educators benefit when they have mentors or supervisors who are interactively engaged with other professionals. The networked access to other perspectives and opinions provides beginners with exposure to other ideas and opinions that can help them shape their own teacher worldview. Community building through face-to-face mentoring, technology integration as a vehicle for dialogue, and networking across groups creates spaces for continuous and robust conversations, problem-solving, and systems change.

Reflective Practice

In addition to the support provided to novice teachers, professional connections allow supervisors to engage in their own reflective practice in ways that acknowledge how others realize their professional responsibilities and how their actions are manifested. This awareness of their impact allows supervisors to better understand how their experiences inform those of the novice educators with whom they work. Reflecting on practice in this way (mentoring as well as teaching practice) prompts supervisors to take action with confidence that their moves result in purposeful outcomes designed to foster teacher learning. An action-oriented approach to mentoring is strengthened by a foundational commitment to reflective practice (Schon, 1983, 1990) and results in agency for mentors who have confidence in their decisions and approaches.

Woven throughout all of these elements of a supervisor with agency is the critical knowledge of best practices and educational contexts. Supervisors who engage their novice educators in learning from practice provide moments of insight that occur through provided advice, suggestions, and reinforcement of best practices around management, instruction, planning, differentiation, etc. When supervisors are able to tailor their support and guidance in response to the nuances of contexts, they are able to inform teachers' work through the application of concepts and skills in ways that are seamlessly applied because supervisors understand the relevant needs of students and community. This understanding is the necessary basis for reflecting on practice, taking action, empowering others, and using voice to make change. Collectively, these skills and approaches are more effective when the supervisor is able to engage through a clear understanding of contexts and best practices for P–12 teaching and learning.

Reviewing the Influence of Supervisor Agency on Professional Practices

As a members of education communities, supervisors bring unique contributions to professional learning in complex settings. To effectively

134   *Conclusion*

impact teacher and P–12 learning, we argue that supervisors with agency: (1) possess a strong understanding of their individual supervisory stance and are able to enact this stance to inform work with novice educators; (2) facilitate professional systems and models that encourage ongoing reflection about practice; (3) utilize advanced communication, collaboration, and relationship skills to encourage agency in teachers; (4) support innovation and best practices with novice educators; and (5) pursue continual learning to improve supervisory practice.

Throughout this text we have illustrated the complexity of education systems and their impact on supervisors' work. We highlight the roles of individuals, their contexts, and the influence of policymaking on teachers' work. To transcend these sometimes limiting features of complex systems, we offer recommendations for supervisors in their ability to empower and lead others through their agency in teacher education.

Chapter 1

In Chapter 1 we presented viewpoints on the purpose of schools and what education stakeholders believe to be the goals for teaching and learning. We have illustrated how these perspectives are informed by personal and community factors, including personal and public histories and policies and procedures for ensuring quality. Supervisors who understand the impact of the layered components of schools and classrooms are therefore in the position to strengthen their influence by situating their roles within complex systems. Knowing and understanding the terrain of education is particularly important for supervisors as alternatives to traditional teacher preparation are on the rise and there are uneven experiences that beginning teachers have had in learning more about educational systems.

A supervisor with agency understands how to inform the work of novices by targeting areas where novices are performing well and areas in need of growth. The knowledge that comes with teaching and an understanding of adult development, reflection on practice, and effective communication are particularly critical when working with traditionally prepared teachers as well as individuals trained through alternative routes. Due to variance in preparation options, attention to overall adequacy of preparation, with a specific focus on diversity, must be a focus of supervisors and early career mentors. Supervisors must provide educators with the skills, knowledge of learners and their contexts, and professional platforms that allow them to engage in critical conversations linked to equity and access. As such, supervisors with agency are able to support innovation and best practices with beginning educators.

Chapter 2

Chapter 2 reviewed the unique features of working with adult learners, recognizing the importance of facilitating experiences and lessons learned

Conclusion 135

that have immediate impact on the real-world problems that educators face daily. Supporting this context, the chapter addressed the history of supervision in teacher education and the resulting mentoring and evaluation practices that have commonly dominated the field. Of crucial importance is the need for professional development experiences that continue professional growth for supervisors.

Agency is developed, in part, through time, experience, and opportunities to interact with others in the same professional roles. When colleges and districts create experiences that foster mentors' reflective connections with self and others, there is space for confidence to act and grow in ways that are professionally empowering. This resulting agency means that there is a further commitment to continued learning—the cycle of reflection and growth will continue to flourish, benefitting supervisors and those they mentor. Powerful professional learning leaves participants wanting more opportunities for continued growth. This is the perfect example that supervisors are attempting to model for novices—learning and growing as a regular part of professional practice, not something that occurs only as a beginner.

Chapter 3

Chapter 3 addressed the influences on supervisors and their prior professional and personal experiences and how they shape supervisory stances toward practice. Agency comes through realizing the impact of these influences on daily supervisory practices. Awareness of one's experiences and how they impart both implicit and explicit knowledge through interaction with novices demonstrates the necessity of understanding stance (Bates et al., 2011). This impacts everything from content knowledge expertise to an understanding of the contextual impacts of classroom, school, and community diversity. Without a clear sense of how biases, assumptions, and personal experiences color the way that supervisors engage in their practice, it is difficult to model reflective standards that are representative of the reflective desires we have for early career educators.

Attending to understanding how classroom diversity and supervisory stance are linked is crucial for ensuring that supervisors reinforce practices that are appropriate for a wide range of P–12 students. As classroom diversity continues to increase across the United States, understanding of supervisors' stances can help them to engage in ways that build their agency along with those of the classroom teachers. Doing so results in a careful use of stance to promote educators' practices that foster welcoming and inclusive classroom communities.

Chapter 4

Chapter 4 highlighted efforts to transform educator communication through contemporary tools that shape technical skill development

136   *Conclusion*

through idea sharing, as well as professional community building. A particular outcome of this effort is the empowerment that educators experience when they take part in an enterprise that exceeds the boundaries of individual classrooms. The knowledge and sense of belonging to a profession-wide commitment informs professional agency by recognizing the power and influence of educators' work. The springboard of community is essential in paving the way for leadership opportunities for both supervisors and in their influence among groups of educators through critical reflections on practice and the profession.

In their roles, supervisors are well suited to invite, foster, and support agency among communities of educators. It is because of the skills and professional agency of the supervisors themselves that those with whom they work experience the ripple effects of professional guidance. The role of supervisors in facilitating professional dialogue and reflection within communities of practice takes place through both traditional and more contemporary strategies for communication. Through the nuanced skills of supervisors educators' agency is enhanced as they build their knowledge base, ability to dialogue locally and beyond, and take a stance in ways that enhance their craft.

Chapter 5

Chapter 5 illustrated the range of ways in which leadership is central to supervisors' work. In addition to the administrative roles assumed by many supervisors, they are in the unique position of guiding others both formally and informally through these positions. Leadership, as a principle, embodies what we believe to be essential for agency among educators. Knowledge of research, precision in skills related to classroom practices, and an awareness of the factors that impact teaching and learning are essential features of leadership. To reach these goals effectively, supervisors must possess the ability to lead as a by-product of effective communication within the context of professional relationships that foster collaborations.

Supervisors who have been prepared and mentored in the skills to effectively guide others are individuals with these critical leadership skills. Whether they remain in classrooms, work within coaching settings, act as university teacher educators, or assume other positions, they are uniquely poised to advance the profession in meaningful ways.

Of crucial importance to supervisory leadership is a clear understanding of the beliefs, attitudes, and understandings that the supervisor uses in practice. The clarity and depth of understanding about supervisory stance is reflected in approaches to leadership. Transparency, both with self and with others, is crucial for this work to have the greatest impact possible on education and educators. Supervisors with agency have a clear stance toward their practice and are able to enact that in leadership roles and settings through guidance, reflection, and action.

Conclusion 137

Chapter 6

Chapter 6 analyzed the impact of supervisors and mentors as one of the tools in the arsenals of teachers and schools to combat the emotional and social pressures of teaching as a profession. Burnout, compassion fatigue, and secondary stress wear on the hearts, minds, and souls of teachers when working with students who have experienced trauma on a regular basis. We explored how supervisors might support the development of resilience in teachers, considering how a supervisor's agency can serve both as a model for the novice educator but also as a voice for resources and supports that are often overlooked with a persistent focus on instructional performance and assessment outcomes. The development of resilience in educators is crucial to ensure that they have the self-care skills to sustain a commitment to the education profession.

Supervisors and mentors play a central role in looking out for the well-being of the teachers they serve, ensuring that the adults in the classroom are cared for as well as the children. This chapter demonstrated the importance of communication, collaboration, and relationship building as avenues to ensure that teachers' needs are known to those with power to help them, ensuring that supervisors' agency can be directed toward the areas of support needed. While all supervisors focus on the instructional aspects of mentoring a novice educator, those with deep understanding of the importance of the emotional health of the teacher recognize the need to direct efforts to ensure care is used. Supervisors with agency have the ability to communicate with both the teacher and others about these needs, with care and tact, while building relationships that foster the teacher's engagement in a community of support. With the increasing challenges of the teaching profession in current times, this is a type of support that cannot be overlooked or underestimated.

Chapter 7

Finally, in Chapter 7 we provided teacher educators and those working with school- and district-level supervisors with guidance on how they may support professional development and training for the supervisors within their schools, universities, and agencies. Our intention is to encourage the technical skills necessary for providing support within the context of supervisors' daily work, while attending to the big picture of education. In all aspects of teacher education, we encourage an approach that recognizes the roles of context, individuals, governance, and equity as among the factors that impact professional practices. Weaving together the many concepts addressed in the text, supervisor agency is foundational to the impact of the profession. Without attending to supervisory agency, the practice is under realized and valuable expertise and experiential learning are lost.

Conclusion

In summary, the proposals presented in this book tout the importance of supervisory agency as an essential component of professional support and advancement for beginning teachers. However, a taken-for-granted assumption in the education profession is that quality supervision happens naturally. Nothing could be further from reality. Without a big picture understanding of teachers' work and the context of education, supervisors and teachers remain as technicians whose work lacks the agency we believe is critical for advancing educational systems. As we have presented, supervisor agency is a catalyst for teachers' work as reflection on and in action (Schon, 1983, 1990). This stance encourages a realistic acceptance that educators must possess technical skill development as well as the critical thinking necessary for today's professionals and that mentors play a foundational role in ensuring that teachers develop in both of these areas.

As those responsible for facilitating supervisor agency, districts, schools, and teacher preparation programs must create opportunities that offer the professional space, time, and necessary resources for engagement in systematic reflection with others, over time, and in ways that are lasting. It is simply not enough to place individuals in supervisory positions. Training, financial support, and professional development create the groundwork for mentoring skills that encourage ongoing reflection about practice. This has the potential to result in supervisor agency enacted in mentoring practices that empower teachers to learn and grow.

In addition to providing adequate resources and fostering a spirit of professional growth, stakeholders must build opportunities that allow for critical masses of supervisors to work together to reach goals that are designed to improve practice and to exert their influence in ways that are lasting. These actions support supervisory agency and equip those in these positions with the professional authority to collaborate and engage with other leaders. The communal element of supervisory agency allows for facilitated decision-making and expanded thinking through dialogue and reflection.

To engage in work that acknowledges the agency and related impact of supervisory work, teacher education programs, district, and schools must hire mentors who bring the knowledge, skills, and disposition to work with novices. Supervisors with agency have the potential to engage novices in powerful learning experiences, changing the shape and nature of educational experiences for P–12 students around the country. Educational systems must embrace the expectation that supervisors need to receive the following: (1) the professional authority to make decisions that support effective practice; (2) a reflection of respect for the role and its complexity, including areas for continued advancement and professional

Conclusion 139

growth; (3) participatory access to make changes in the mentoring of novices that can support growth in both the individual and the system; and (4) time and space to do the hard work of mentoring with attention to the needs of each individual novice educator.

Taken collectively, supervision and mentoring have the power to make a difference for each teacher. Building the capacity to support supervisors' agency is a worthwhile cost and effort for districts and universities to ensure the success of teachers. The stakes continue to rise for all involved with the increasing accountability and assessment of professional practices combined with the diversification of the P–12 student population. Empowering supervisors with agency to engage in the most deeply meaningful ways to build practice is time and effort well spent.

References

American Association of Colleges of Teacher Education. (2013). *The changing teacher preparation profession: A report from AACTE's Professional Education Data System (PEDS)*. Washington, DC: Author.

American Association of Colleges of Teacher Education. (2018). *A pivot toward clinical practice, its lexicon, and the renewal of educator preparation*. Washington, DC: Author.

Bates, A. J., & Burbank, M. D. (2008). Effective student teacher supervision in the era of *No Child Left Behind. The Professional Educator, 32*(2), 1–11.

Bates, A. J., Drits, D., & Ramirez, L. (2011). Self-awareness and enactment of supervisory stance: Influences on responsiveness toward student teacher learning. *Teacher Education Quarterly, 38*(3), 69–87.

Bates, A. J., Ramirez, L., & Drits, D. (2009). Critical reflection in university supervision: Mentoring and modeling. *The Teacher Educator, 44*(2), 1–23.

Bates, A. J., & Rosaen, C. L. (2010). Making sense of classroom diversity: Supports for interns' learning about students through field instruction practices. *Studying Teacher Education, 6*(1), 45–61.

Burbank, M. D., Bates, A. J., & Gupta, U. (2016). The influence of teacher development on secondary content area supervision among preservice teachers. *The Teacher Educator, 51*(1), 55–69.

Burbank, M. D., Ramirez, L., & Bates, A. J. (2012). Critically reflective thinking in urban teacher education: A comparative case study of two participants' experiences as content specialists. *The Professional Educator, 36*(2).

Gallavan, N., & Webster-Smith, A. (2012). Commentary. In R. Flessner, G. R. Miller, K. M. Patrizio, & J. R. Horwitz (Eds.), *Agency through teacher education: Reflection, community, and learning*. New York, NY: Rowman & Littlefield Education.

Levine, T. H. (2011). Features and strategies of supervisor professional community as a means of improving the supervisor of student teachers. *Teaching and Teacher Education, 27*, 930–941.

Rust, F. O., & Freidus, H. (Eds.). (2001). *Guiding school change: The role of work of change agents*. New York, NY: Teachers College Press.

140 *Conclusion*

Schön, D. A. (1983). *The reflective practitioner: How professionals think in action.* New York, NY: Basic Books.

Schön, D. A. (1990). *Educating the reflective practitioner: Toward a new design for teaching and learning in the profession.* San Francisco, CA: Jossey-Bass.

Zeichner, K. (2012). The turn once again toward practice-based teacher education. *Journal of Teacher Education, 63*(5), 376–382.

Zeichner, K. (2017). *The struggle for the soul of teacher education.* Abingdon, UK: Routledge.

Index

AACTE 121
accountability 8, 33, 56
accreditation: mandates 14, 77; national and state 123; requirements 14
action research 19, 121–122
activities: action research and self-study 121–122; evaluating supervisory feedback 123–124; professional development 113
adult learners 6, 42; facilitating growth and reflection in 26; needs of 26; understanding 27–28; working with 134–135
adult learning, four principles for 28
adverse childhood experiences (ACEs) study 101
agency: development of 135; effecting change through 109; enacting with novice teachers 7; enactments of by teacher educators 6; as learning 6; and resilience 106–109; *see also* supervisor/supervisory agency; teacher agency
agency and ownership, promoting 36–37
agency in supervisors: defined 3–9; *see also* supervisor/supervisory agency
alternate routes to licensure (ARL) 15, 85
American Association of Colleges of Teacher Education (AACTE) 116, 121
American Educational Research Association (AERA) 120–121
andragogy 27–28, 42; assumptions that guide 27; and PLC structure 39; recommendations for 27

ARL programs 15, 85
audio feedback 72

beliefs: biased 76; manifested in daily work 118; of preservice teacher supervisors 17; and practice 117
book clubs 40
burnout 36, 47, 100, 103–104, 137; coping mechanisms 105, 106; and younger teachers 107

CFGs *see* critical friends groups
change agents: and context 5; contextual knowledge of 6; learning curve 6; as nurturers 6; roles of 5–6
childhood trauma 101
classroom diversity 16–17, 47, 57; and candidate readiness to teach 59; and content area expectations 57; recognizing elements of 57; role of communities and families 16
classroom observations 13, 33
clinical pedagogy 34
clinical supervision model 29–30
cloud storage 75
coaches 7; effective 92; instructional 91–92; self-reports of supervisory characteristics 92–93; and transformational approach 93
coaching 7, 91; styles 93
Cognitive Coaching 91
collaboration 28, 38–39, 51, 95; and book clubs 40; between schools and universities 54; and negotiation 5; online 69; in special education settings 72; with supervision peers 120; and technology 64
collaborative decision-making 95
collaborative mentoring practice 36

142　*Index*

collaborative reflection 52
communication etiquette 72
community building 70–71, 133, 136; within classrooms and schools 88
community of practice 39, 95, 108
compassion fatigue 100, 103, 104, 106, 137; mentor's response to 105
compassion satisfaction 106; and resilience 107
complex stance 51–52
confidentiality 74–75
connectedness 7, 132–133
content area 48; conventions 34; expectations and classroom diversity 57; expertise 19; influence of 55–57; supervision 34
content expertise, role in supervisory practice 55
content innovation 55
content knowledge 19, 34–35; evaluations 13; expertise 60; and pedagogy 55–56
context/contexts 1, 2, 12: and change agents 5; educational 119–120; role in classrooms 79; role of 131; supervisors' work within 19–20
contextual knowledge 6
contextual supervision 58
cooperating teacher 59
cooperating teacher: beliefs 52; and content innovation 55; and student teacher relationships 53; influence on student teaching experience 52–54
Council for Accreditation in Education Preparation 14
critical discourse 58
critical friends groups 40–42
critical reflection 6, 49, 118; critically reflective practices 13, 47; *see also* reflection
critical thinking 79, 117
culturally responsive: classroom practices 58–59; supervision 57–59
culture of schools 58, 109, 119–120
curriculum change 6
curriculum development 4

data-based decision-making 14, 88
data-driven performance indicators 13
decision-making: collaborative 95; community-based 88; through virtual mentoring 69–70
developmental supervision 31–32

dialogic praxis 36
dialogue 35–36, 68; within educational communities 76; goal of professional dialogue 117–118; and technology 64; professional 131
distributed leadership 90
diverse student populations 34; *see also* classroom diversity
diversity 132; in educator communities 72–73; *see also* classroom diversity

early career mentor *see* university supervisor
early career teacher mentor 7, 27, 33, 108; *see also* mentors; supervisors; university supervisors
early career mentoring models 32–33
e-communities 69; *see also* electronic communities
e-conversations 65
edTPA 78
education: and community dynamics 12; perceptions of in the United States 12; public attitudes on 12
educative mentoring 27, 32, 37
educator communities, diverse 72–73
developmental differences among educators 18
electronic communities 68, 72–73; benefits of 71; *see also* e-communities
electronic portfolios 77–78
electronic readers 70, 71
electronic spaces 73, 79
electronic supervision, for skill and community building 70–71
elementary supervisors 55
e-mentoring 68
empowerment 132; of educators 95; of mentors/supervisors 34, 35, 39, 42, 56; and resilience 107–108; of teacher candidates 56; of teachers 3, 4, 40
equity 16–17, 34, 48, 58, 90
e-readers 70, 71
e-supervision, and video storytelling 78–79
evaluation conferences 33
experiences, role in adult learning 27, 28

Facebook 75
face-to-face mentoring 68

Index 143

Family Educational Rights and Privacy Act (FERPA) 74
feedback 2, 19, 35, 58, 64, 68; audio 72; in critical friends groups 41; evaluating 123–124; in online environments 71, 75; by peers 67; and reflection 71; types of 71; video 66, 67; virtual 65–68
formal leadership 89

graduate student 50
group dynamic 122; within supervisory relationships 70

horizontal supervision 30–31

individual histories, reflection on 115–116
informal leadership 89
initiative 54
innovation 55
instructional coaches 91–92; impact of 94–95
isolation 38, 69, 95, 108

justificatory discourse 58

knowledge of self 59
knowledge transformation 32, 37

leadership: coaches' engagement in 93; communities 89; cultivating 90; and decision-making 88, 90; distributed 90; educational 89–90; facilitation of teacher leadership 86; informal 89; organized style of 90; role in education 89; roles for teachers 88–89; school-based 89; skills 92; supervisors as change agents 86; supervisors as school leaders 84–89; supervisory 95, 131, 136; unplanned leadership positions 85; *see also* teacher leaders
leadership styles: coaches' beliefs regarding 92–93; data on perceptions of 92–93; employing transformational practices 92–93
legislation 13
lesson plans 20, 33
lexicon 7–8

marginalized students 16
mentor agency 32–33, 35

mentoring 1; attention to reflection 37; early career teachers 32–33; supervisors as change agents for 2–3; virtual 67
mentoring models 32–33
mentors 30, 42; and adult learners 27; as adult learners 26, 115; for early career teachers 36, 49; facilitating teacher leadership 86; and guided practice 19; individual histories 115–116; informal roles 91; and leadership 84–89; need for professional development 84; pedagogical skills 33; at the preservice level 19–20; providing alternatives to improve teaching 19; qualities that increase autonomy 92; relationships with novice educators 6; relationships with school/district leaders 109–110; stakeholders in teacher preparation 114–115; support for 38; as teachers for equity 16–17; understanding contexts 12; varied roles of 87; *see also* supervisors
mentors and teachers, conflicting demands 14
multilayered system of training 94–95

National Council on Teacher Quality 13
NBPTS portfolio model 78
negotiation 5, 53–54
novice teachers 18–19
nurturing 6

observation cycle 2
observational feedback, in critical friends groups 41
one-on-one mentoring 1, 41
online collaboration 69
Online Community Network system 71
online mentoring 67
orientation to learning 27–28

P–12 classrooms, evaluating teacher quality in 13–14
P–12 student performance, factors impacting 14
partnership models 54
PBIS 91
pedagogical decisions, guidance by supervisors 47

144 *Index*

pedagogical skills 33–34
pedagogy 19, 27; in the elementary classroom 55; and content 55–57
performance assessment 77; and portfolio development 125; standardized 77; technology and 76–78
performance-based assessments 76–77; via portfolios 77–78
perseverance 109–110
Personal Learning Networks (PLN) 73
perspectives: building 78–79; on goals for teaching and learning 134; of preservice teacher supervisors 17; from professional communities 118–119; regarding supervision 117
perspective-taking 69, 116, 117; experiences 76; and teacher agency 68
policy reviews 123
portfolios 77–78, 115, 125
positive behavioral interventions and support (PBIS) 91
practicum experiences, purposes of 116–117
preservice teachers, individual histories 115–116
privacy 74–75
problem-solving 28, 88, 92; and virtual mentoring 67
professional development 17, 39, 51; support for 137; and technology 65
professional learning communities (PLCs) 38, 39–40, 95, 122
professional organizations 120–121

questioning 35–36, 41–42

readiness to learn 27
reflecting on practice 133
reflection 3, 18–19, 117; collaborative 52; and critical friends groups 42; and feedback 71; impact on teaching 18; *in action* 37; in practice 37; *on action* 37; on practice 37, 51, 52, 79; prompts for 117, 118, 121, 124; purpose and promotion of in teacher preparation 37–38; and technology 67; through virtual mentoring 69–70; *see also* critical reflection
reflective learning 54
reflective models 30

reflective practice(s) 18, 30, 133
reflective thinking 57, 58
reflective work 60; *see also* reflection; reflective practices; reflective thinking
renegotiation 53–54
research, and educational practitioners 120–122
research organizations 120–121
research project 122
resilience: and agency 106–109; building 100, 108–109; in children 100, 101; and control 107; development of in teachers 106, 137; and perseverance 109–110; and relationships 102; of teachers 102–103; and teacher-student relationship 102; and trauma 101–102
retention of teachers 16, 37, 85
rubrics 33, 72, 78; electronic 77

school contexts, role of 131
school culture 58, 109, 119–120
school histories 119
school improvement models 3
schools, purpose(s) of 11–12
secondary education, supervision in 55–56
secondary stress 100, 103, 137
secondary traumatic stress 104, 106; coping mechanisms 105
self-awareness 51
self-concept, changes in 27
self-reflection, systematic 121–122
self-study 121–122; of practice 42
"shifting" 56, 57
silencing response 104
situated cognition 39
situated learning 69
situational teaching 31–32
social factors 35
social justice 17, 48
social media 73–74; anonymity 75; ethical considerations 75; information sharing on 75–76; practical considerations 74–75; privacy and confidentiality 74–75; users' perceptions of autonomy 75–76
special education 72–73
stance 7, 37, 50, 114, 118; impact on supervision 51–52

Index 145

standardization 4
standardized performance assessment 77; and refection potential 78
storytelling 78–79, 115
student diversity *see* classroom diversity
student teachers 56, 57; as adult learners 26; mentoring of 1
student teaching, purposes of 116–117
supervision: culturally responsive 48, 57–59; effective 7, 33; five-stage model of 30; impact of supervisory stance on 51–52; and intersection of influences 8, 48; of newly hired teachers 1; of preservice teachers 48; research on 28–29
supervision as leadership, developing potential for 93–95
supervision portfolio 125
supervisors 2, 12–13, 67–68; and agency-building 37; beliefs regarding their work 116–118; bridging theory and practice 49; building professional relationships 12–13; as change agents 2–3; and diversity 17; and direct feedback 19; evolution of 50; individual histories 115–116; and leadership 84–89; models for support of 38–42; as negotiators 5, 59; pedagogical skills 33; personal and professional history 48–51; professional development 34, 49, 50–51; relationships in school settings 132–133; relationship with school/district leaders 109–110; as stakeholders in teacher preparation 114–115; support for early career teachers 36; as teachers for equity 16–17; theory and practice 34; in triadic relationship 52; voice and empowerment 132; *see also* mentors; university supervisors
supervisors as leaders: characteristics of 92–93; skills and dispositions 90–91
supervisor/supervisory agency 7, 31, 57, 72, 138; facilitating 132–133; influence on professional practices 133–137; and support of novice educators 107

supervisors' work: within complex and layered contexts 19–20; with preservice teachers 93–94; science and art of 131
supervisory episodes, recording and assessing 123–124
supervisory feedback, evaluating 123–124
supervisory practice 56; common strategies 33–36; effect of previous professional development 51
supervisory relationships 58; 69
supervisory stance 7, 114, 135; impact on supervision 51–52
supervisory support 56, 66, 131; complexity of 47–48; electronic 71; strategies 56–57; using virtual storage 75
supervisory work with beginning teachers, areas of 114

teacher: effectiveness 13–14; knowledge 87
teacher agency: and action 4; concept of 3; conceptualizations of agency in 6–7; counteracting burnout 106–107; development of 2; and perspective-taking 68
teacher development, research on 18
teacher education 1; encouraging agency 47; supervision in 28–29
teacher educators, delineation of roles 116
teacher leaders 115; media depictions of 86; work of 85
teacher practices, developing 131
teacher preparation: change in 85; determining programmatic impact 13; expectations for 15; and reflection 37–38; trends 14–16; in the United States 11–20
teacher preparation programs 114; alternative 15; dimensions of 122–123; and standards 123
teacher/teaching quality: assessment practices 13–14; data-based decision-making of 14; efforts to measure 13; evaluating in P–12 classrooms 13–14; methods to determine 76–77
teacher research 4
teachers and mentors, conflicting demands 14

146 *Index*

teacher shortages 84–85; and ARL programs 15

teacher supervision: evolution of 29; influences on 11

teacher supervisors 67; demographic 17; *see also* supervisors

teachers' work 87, 138; assessment and evaluation of 13–14; documentation of 77; human side of 72; overlooked components 12; research on 120; role of reflection in 18–19; and supervisory support 113–114

teaching: adaptive expertise 1; alternative routes to 15; support for success 16; technical components 12

teaching episodes 19; review of 65, 66, 67, 77, 79

technology and performance assessment, opportunities and challenges 76–78

technology infusion: electronic formats in supervisory practices 66; and dialogue 69; and reflection 65, 69; and supervisors 65

technology: and professional development 65; and reflection 67

technology integration in education, history of 64–65

technology integration in supervision 64, 71, 79; capturing teaching episodes 66; dedicated skills for 71–73; goals and uses of 64–65; opportunities and challenges 66–67; and teacher anxiety 66; Twitter as a supervisory tool 74; virtual communities of practice 67–69;

virtual supervision and mentoring 69–70

tiered support 94–95

training, multilayered system 94–95

transformational approach, and leadership style 93

transformational practices 93

trauma 100; defined 101; impacts on teachers 103–105; and resilience 101–102; support for supervisors and mentors 105

triadic relationships 52–54, 59

turnover 103, 109

Twitter 73–74

university supervision 2

university supervisors 7, 54, 59; and adult learners 27, 28–29; building resilience 108; development of relationships 59; isolation 38; professional growth 50; role of 2, 26, 50; in triadic relationship 53

video: recording supervisory episodes 123; reviews 77; storytelling 78–79

video-based evaluations 19

video systems 66, 67

virtual communities: information sharing in 75–76; of practice 67–69

virtual dialogue/discussion 68, 70

virtual feedback 65–67

virtual mentoring 67–68

virtual supervision and mentoring: and group support 70; and interpersonal dimensions 69–70; reflection and decision-making 69–70; support 68

voice 7, 58, 68, 132